e learned to trust Andy Andrews to bring words of inspiration, cal instruction, and wise counsel. This volume promises to bring me to all who are blessed to read it."

—Max Lucado, pastor and *New York Times* bestselling author

n thrilled the material in *The Bottom of the Pool* is now available for yone. Fearless Mom has used Andy's information and insights as part r core learning. In just one year our subscribers grew by 233 percent, we are now reaching moms in more than thirty countries. This book provide direction for you as a parent and lead you to answers in your sonal and professional life."

—Julie Richard, Fearless Mom founder

/ith his words, Andy Andrews shapes creative thought in a way that anges lives."

—Muriel T. Summers, Principal of the Year, A. B. Combs Magnet Elementary School, twice named America's Best Elementary School

This book could not be more valuable if the words had been printed on olid gold paper. Three years ago my business had stalled at a moderate evel of success, and I couldn't figure out how to get it growing again. Then found Andy Andrews and his principles from *The Bottom of the Pool.* Since putting these principles into practice, my business has grown by more than 500 percent. In addition, there's one specific teaching included in this book that directly brought in more than $700,000 in revenue."

—Tiffany King, Eat at Home and Eat at Home Meal Plans owner and author, *Eat at Home Tonight*

PRAISE FO

THE BOTTOM OF T

"In the first year of our relationship with Andy Andr
its business volume—from $5.4 billion to $11.2 bill
with Andy, we cracked $17 billion, and the third
$22 billion."

—Steve Jacobson, Fairway Independent
Mortgage Corporation founder and CEO

"I remember the day Andy Andrews said he could teac
a level our competition didn't know existed. That was i
counsel we quickly passed the $100 million mark. This
ducing at a level 338 percent higher than our closest comp

—Todd Rainsberger, Coldwell Banker Comm
Real Estate owner and broker

"For five years we were the *only* corporation in our i
taught the material now included in *The Bottom of the*
was Andy Andrews the only outside influence consiste
with our sales professionals, but he also mentored our ex
During that period, we went from less than $100 millio
revenue to ten times that amount. When Andy first spoke
him in front of an audience of eight hundred. Five years l
grown to a point that the same event was held in Cowboys

—Richard Wright, Advocare International
former president and CEO

"Andy Andrews is America's best storyteller since Mark Twain. Who knew laughter and insight would be such an incredible combination?"

—Mark Lowry, artist and songwriter of the Christmas classic *Mary, Did You Know?*

"I am writing these words at the end of January 2019. Yes, I did receive early access to the material included in *The Bottom of the Pool,* and my business has been utilizing the methods outlined in this book. Amazingly, we have already increased our 2019 results by 51 percent over last year at this time. If you read one book this year, make it this one. *The Bottom of the Pool* will make sense to you in a way no book ever has."

—Joe Pici, Pici & Pici Inc. president and CEO, named to Global Gurus's World's Top 30 Sales Professionals

"With the publication of *The Bottom of The Pool,* I am now convinced that Andy Andrews is in a category of one. Whether the advancement you seek is personal or professional, this book will greatly apply to your situation. What you have heard is true: Andy Andrews produces astonishing results."

—Dave Ramsey, radio host and bestselling author, *The Total Money Makeover*

OTHER BOOKS BY ANDY ANDREWS

NOVELS

Return to Sawyerton Springs

The Heart Mender

The Lost Choice

The Noticer

The Noticer Returns

The Traveler's Gift

The Traveler's Summit

NONFICTION

How Do You Kill 11 Million People?

The Little Things

The Seven Decisions

The Traveler's Gift Journal

YOUNG ADULT

The Young Traveler's Gift

CHILDREN'S AND GIFT

Baseball, Boys, and Bad Words

The Butterfly Effect

Henry Hodges Needs a Friend

The Kid Who Changed the World

The Perfect Moment

Socks for Christmas

The BOTTOM of the POOL

THINKING **BEYOND** YOUR **BOUNDARIES** TO ACHIEVE **EXTRAORDINARY RESULTS**

ANDY ANDREWS

W PUBLISHING GROUP

AN IMPRINT OF THOMAS NELSON

Published in Nashville, Tennessee, by W Publishing Group, an imprint of Thomas Nelson.

Thomas Nelson titles may be purchased in bulk for educational, business, fund-raising, or sales promotional use. For information, please e-mail SpecialMarkets@ThomasNelson.com.

ISBN 978-0-7852-2654-3 (eBook)

Library of Congress Cataloging-in-Publication Data

Names: Andrews, Andy, 1959– author.
Title: The bottom of the pool : thinking beyond your boundaries to achieve extraordinary results / Andy Andrews.
Description: Nashville : W Publishing Group, 2019. |
Identifiers: LCCN 2018058215 (print) | LCCN 2019012872 (ebook) | ISBN 9780785226543 (Ebook) | ISBN 9780785226536 (hardback)
Subjects: LCSH: Success. | Self-realization.
Classification: LCC BF637.S8 (ebook) | LCC BF637.S8 A517 2019 (print) | DDC 158.1—dc23
LC record available at https://lccn.loc.gov/2018058215

Printed in the United States of America

19 20 21 22 23 LSC 6 5 4 3 2 1

Dedicated to those of you who are a
part of my life's "shield wall."
You are the most valuable of friends, holding
me up when I was unable to stand. And
during the time I couldn't move at all, you
stepped forward and surrounded me.

CONTENTS

One
THE GAME

When I was a kid, my parents would drop me off at the pool during the summer. This must've been an excellent childcare method because most of my friends' parents did the same thing. Day after day, all summer long, we never seemed to tire of being "at the pool." Though we were almost always *in* the pool, for some reason, that is how we referred to being there.

"Where were you yesterday?"

"At the pool."

We played Marco Polo, horse and rider, water football, atomic whirlpool, watermelon push, and blue rover—which was just like red rover except that it was in the water. Back then, of course, all swimming pools were treated with vast amounts of chlorine. By the middle of July, if a blond kid didn't have a lime-green tint to his hair, it was obvious to everyone he hadn't spent much time at the pool.

Another thing would happen about the middle of July. We would become somewhat bored with much of what we had been doing and begin to invent our own games.

One year we created a contest we called "Dolphin." At the time, everyone loved the television show *Flipper*, which was about a dolphin who was involved in one adventure after another. (Think Lassie in a wet suit.) The human stars of the show were Bud and Sandy, the sons of a park ranger in Coral Key National Park.

There was no one our age who didn't watch the show, and all of us were amazed at how Flipper could lift straight up out of the water and "walk" on his tail.

So that was our game.

We'd all form a big circle in the deep end of the pool, everyone treading water. One at a time, we would take turns being the dolphin. Each person in turn swam to the center of the circle. The object of the game was to use your arms, legs, hands, and feet to lift your torso out of the water as high as you could.

No one ever got as much air as Aaron Perry. He was older than most of us by a year and almost a head taller. Believe me when I say that it was tough to compete against his big feet. And his hands . . . Oh my gosh, his hands! No child has ever had hands that big. I'm telling you, the kid could palm a basketball in the third grade!

Aaron's physical structure was a decided advantage in the pool. When Aaron flapped his massive feet and waved those catcher's mitts he called hands to push against the water, the kid would rise above the pool's surface like Flipper himself. Or at least like Flipper's human cousin.

It was the summer after our fourth-grade year, and most of us were eleven years old. Aaron, obviously, was twelve. He told us quite often that he was better than we were at everything. Unfortunately, we were convinced he was right. It was depressing.

At Dolphin, particularly, Aaron *was* the best. He always won. Always. His winning streak (which, of course, began with the invention of the game) was unprecedented. Undefeated, untied, unrivaled, and in a water-treading circle of fourth-going-on-fifth-graders, unapproachable. He was unapologetically unbelievable. And he knew it. Aaron was the king of Dolphin!

Until the day Kevin Perkins beat him by a foot and a half.

I remember that afternoon like it was yesterday. There were about ten of us in the deep end. We were in a loose circle, each taking our turn and watching closely as everyone else took theirs. We were not only competitors; we rotated our responsibility as judges. All of us had equal say, but despite trying to be fair, disagreements were routine.

That day, I'd already taken my turn. So, too, had Aaron and everyone else except for Kevin Perkins, my best friend. As Kevin swam to the center of the circle, several of the kids called out, "Hurry up. Do it. Get it over with."

Two of our group—Roger Luker and his girlfriend, Carol—even left early. Not that I blamed them. Had there been an Azalea Pool Dolphin Historical Record for anyone to examine, it would have shown quite clearly that after Aaron Perry took his turn, the game was over. On the other hand, everyone liked Kevin, so most of the kids waited. We waited somewhat impatiently, but we waited.

Kevin paused in the center. "Ready?" he called.

"Yes!" we responded. "Just go!"

And he did. But he did not go up. Kevin went down.

Those of us left on the surface shot questioning looks at one another. What was he doing? We treaded water a little harder trying to see him below us. Kevin had gone all the way to the bottom. He was bending his knees . . . squatting, going lower . . . getting as close to the bottom as he could.

Suddenly, before any of us had time to pose a question or make a comment, Kevin pushed hard off the concrete and headed for the surface, coming fast. A second after he left the bottom, Kevin burst up and into the air with a triumphant yell.

We yelled too. It was plain to see that Kevin had gone much higher than Aaron had ever managed. What a moment! It was thrilling. It wasn't long, though, before Aaron said, "Well, sure you went higher, but what you did . . . well, that's not the way you do it. You cheated."

Kevin smiled calmly. "Really?" he replied. "And ahh . . . where's the rule that says you can't go down before you go up?"

"Yeah! Yeah!" we agreed excitedly. "Where's *that* rule? Huh? Huh?" We splashed water in Aaron's face again and again. The old chlorinated-water-in-the-eyes maneuver, along with the implied threat of at least a half dozen eleven-year-olds holding his head underwater (and other forms of preadolescent swimming-pool violence), Aaron quickly agreed that Kevin's new technique *was* legal.

Unfortunately the Official Dolphin League Rules Committee—Danny Stone and Bob Woodall—were forced (by

Aaron's mother) to concede that the new technique would be immediately available to all competitors in future contests.

As Aaron would use the new method in our very next game, everyone knew the crown would not be Kevin's for very long. Interestingly, however, it was Kevin's breakthrough that we all remembered and revered. By changing our understanding and belief about what was possible, Kevin had actually changed the game. Forever.

Though Aaron was once again the proud king of Dolphin, it was Kevin's solitary win—that one incredible leap into the air—that we all remembered. To us, Kevin is still the Dolphin legend.

As the passing years turned into passing decades, it became curious to me how often my mind drifted back to that particular day. And every time I recalled the event, the memories arrived with an uncertain cloud around the edges. It was as if I had forgotten something.

Maybe I *didn't* forget, I mused one day. Maybe I missed something entirely. But what could I have missed? I was right beside Kevin when it happened. I saw everything. And the story has never changed.

Still, there was some unanswered something, an unidentified thought, the hangnail of an idea that would not leave me alone. Finally, one morning several years ago, I woke up with this: during the entire history of the game Dolphin—until the moment Kevin Perkins rocketed out of the water—every one of us had competed every single time in the exact same way.

Exactly the same way? Yes. Why? Because we knew how the game was played. We *knew* how it was done. It is an odd thought to consider, but because Azalea Pool was the only place in the world our game was being played, we were not merely experts. No, in actual fact—though we were children—we were the best Dolphin players on the planet.

By changing our understanding and belief about what was possible, Kevin had actually changed the game. Forever.

Unfortunately, there exists a principle that none of us understood at the time. Even long into adulthood, I never imagined it existed. The principle governs Limits and Results and holds absolute sway over every part of your life. The principle is at the same time incredibly simple and unbelievably mind boggling. It goes like this:

> **Be careful about what you think you know.**
> **Because you can't always believe everything you think.**

Two

A GLIMMER OF UNDERSTANDING

So we were the best Dolphin players on the planet.

The fact that we were the *only* players on the planet makes no difference.

And ponder this: if we were the best and Aaron was the best among us, then Aaron Perry was the single best Dolphin player in existence!

For the rest of us, our methods—what we did in practice and in games—were virtually identical to the methods Aaron employed. We faithfully studied and carefully mimicked his every move. Our reason for doing so was no mystery. We did what Aaron did because of his success. Aaron Perry was the sport's gold standard. That fact was beyond dispute.

Even when he was not at the pool, Aaron was in our heads. We thought about him constantly. We held secret discussions to dissect everything Aaron did in what always turned out to be another fruitless effort to divine the magic in his results.

How, we wondered, did the big man cup his hands and at what angle? Did he tuck his thumb under his fingers and into his palm? Or was his thumb placed *beside* his fingers? Did Aaron flutter his feet continuously as he rose into the air, or was it *one big kick* that propelled him to such lofty heights?

None of us possessed the physical advantages that Aaron had (Good grief, the kid was a giant! He was almost four foot ten!), but because we were able to observe him so closely day after day, we began to perfect his moves, and, as a result, our own performances steadily improved.

We had already been playing the game for a couple of years. As we learned and grew physically, several of us actually progressed to the point that we came pretty darn close to Aaron's results. But Aaron was growing and improving, too, and for that reason, at least until Kevin's big surprise, we never beat him.

Decades have passed since that summer, yet none of us have forgotten the day my best friend used the bottom of the pool as a foundation for greatness. At first, when Kevin went down instead of up, we thought he had lost his mind, but he continued all the way to the bottom. Kevin, it turned out, had sensed a power to be harnessed, one that would produce results the rest of us had never suspected were possible.

Though he had purposely moved in a direction that was totally opposite from the accepted approach to the game, Kevin employed a strategy that had never been tried before, and the results he achieved not only proved his instincts correct, but they changed the game forever.

> Kevin, it turned out, had sensed a power to be harnessed, one that would produce results the rest of us had never suspected were possible.

Kevin Perkins was eleven years old, but at Azalea Pool that afternoon when he broke the surface of the water—clenched fists held high; a mighty yell from the depths of his soul—that moment, to everyone who witnessed it, could only be described as Beamonesque.

Beamonesque? Absolutely.

Three

A MIND HAS WINGS?

Whether or not you are familiar with the word *Beamonesque*, rest assured that it is an actual word that is included in several dictionaries. That the word is not in *all* dictionaries is due to the fact that until October 18, 1968, there would have been no reason to add "esque" to the name Beamon.

The year was 1968. Gasoline was twenty-eight cents per gallon, Apollo astronauts were orbiting the moon, and *The Andy Griffith Show* filmed its last episode, ending its final season at number one in the ratings, still only one of three television series to accomplish that feat, the other two being *I Love Lucy* and *Seinfeld*.

Surely it was coincidence, but in 1968—the same year Kevin became the Dolphin legend—a young man named Bob Beamon was verging on immortality in the world of track and field. Not that anyone suspected it.

The results he was posting were excellent, though not excellent enough to suspect the greatness to come. Originally from Queens, New York, he competed in only one event . . . the long jump.

Beamon was headed to the Olympic Games in Mexico City and considered a possible medal contender. Unfortunately, the two days of competition for which he had physically prepared his entire life did not begin well. He jumped poorly throughout both days. Close to elimination in the preliminaries, Beamon almost missed the finals completely, not qualifying until his third and last attempt.

In the finals with Beamon on that second day were the two previous long jump gold medalists: American Ralph Boston, who had won the event in 1960, and Lynn Davies from Great Britain, the winner in 1964.

Rounding out the field of competitors was Igor Ter-Ovanesyan. Ter-Ovanesyan was born in Kiev to an Armenian discus-thrower father and Ukrainian volleyball-player mother and competed on the Soviet Olympic team. Twice, he had won Olympic bronze medals. At *these* Olympics, however, it was the Soviet athlete who came into Mexico City as the favorite to win gold, for he was the current holder of the world record in long jump.

A year earlier, at an international meet held in the same Mexico City stadium, he had set the record against the same three competitors—Boston, Davies, and Beamon—he was now facing on the world's biggest stage, the finals of the Olympic Games.

In a century of competition prior to those 1968 Olympics, the world record in long jump had been broken only thirteen times. The increase, when the record *was* broken, averaged a mere two and a half inches. On the day of the Olympic finals, the world record still stood where the Soviet had placed it the year before—27 feet, 4.75 inches. Davies led out, followed by Boston, then Ter-Ovanesyan. The first three competitors' attempts landed each of them just shy of the twenty-seven-foot mark.

Having done what they could, the three turned to watch the young American. On an impulse, however, Ralph Boston moved quickly to Beamon's side. Considering himself a mentor to the younger athlete, Boston spoke directly into Beamon's left ear. Years passed before either man described the momentary one-sided conversation, but in that instant, Bob Beamon was transformed by an almost supernatural focus he had never before experienced.

Later he would reflect upon that moment and the words of his friend. "Physically," Beamon said, "I was as close to perfect as I ever got. Mentally . . . and I didn't know this, of course . . . I was not nearly so strong. But as I stood there, about to approach the track for my jump, Ralph spoke to me. His words took shape in my head."

Archival footage of those seconds reveals a stoic Beamon staring straight ahead as Boston urgently spoke to him. Quickly, the older athlete whispered, "Take off early. You have room to spare. Give 'em two inches on the front. You'll take two feet when you land. Your legs have never been as strong as they are right now. At this moment your body weighs nothing. Your mind has wings. Use them. Fly up. Fly out."

Boston backed away and Beamon moved into position. For twenty seconds, he stared down the track. Rocking back only once, he shot forward with his head up and his arms pumping like pistons.

Astonishingly, it took a scant six seconds for Beamon to take nineteen hard strides, leap to a height of more than six feet into the air—his legs continuing to wheel forward in a running motion—and land in the sand pit at the end of the track.

But there was a problem . . .

The issue was not with Beamon's takeoff, the most likely foul for long jumpers who often overstep the starting board. He also landed cleanly inside the boundaries of the sand pit.

The predicament was caused by *where* the American had landed in the sand pit. The optical device that had been installed by the IOC to measure distances failed to measure his leap. Bob Beamon had jumped over and well beyond it.

For almost twenty minutes, the entire stadium watched, waiting impatiently as the Olympic judges located an old-fashioned tape measure in order to make an official ruling about what had just occurred.

When the distance was finally posted, there was a stunned silence on the field and in the stadium. Within seconds, Beamon fell to his knees, his face in his hands, and there began a roar from the crowd that literally shook the building.

Bob Beamon had jumped 29 feet, 2.5 inches—almost two feet beyond what any person had ever done.

Beamon didn't simply set a record; he shattered it. That Olympic record still stands today, and most agree with the assessment made on the spot by Lynn Davies, the defending Olympic gold medalist. "Bob," he said in awe, "you have destroyed the event!"

"The Jump," as it came to be known, was named by *Sports Illustrated* as one of the five greatest sports moments of the twentieth century. ESPN named it the most amazing Olympic performance in history. And as you already know, that one jump by the young man from New York so stunned the world that it created its own word:

> *Beamonesque* . . . an adjective meaning "a result so far superior to anything accomplished before, it is overwhelming."

Four

BEFORE WE CONTINUE

With an eye on our ultimate destination—the bottom of the pool—and an understanding that its greatest benefits accrue in the lives of those who can regularly make the trip, for now I only encourage a first step. It's time to get our faces wet and take a quick peek below the surface.

When you think about it, even though you and I will venture only a few inches underwater for now, those few inches are in fact a slightly deeper place in the pool than most people traditionally inhabit.

Most?

Yes, most. Through the years, I have come to my own conclusion about what percentage of people constitutes "most." In reality, especially regarding this particular area of thought, *most* could mean anything from 51 to 99 percent.

So what do I think *most* means? I'm afraid it is not my place to tell you—at least not now. I am your servant on this journey, your compass bearer. As your guide to this rarely visited place, I know too well that human nature will probably not allow you to be taken by the arm and shown the way more than once. This is why I usually answer questions . . . with a question.

My greatest value to you at this time is not to simply tell you what I think! If I did, *my* conclusion would quickly find a home in *your* head. Once it's filed away, your brain would label it "The Answer," and, just like that, a barrier would have been created, preventing you from thinking beyond what I—and now you—already know.

Instead, I will illustrate effective strategies that you can apply in your own search for wisdom. These will include true examples of results that have been gained by perfectly ordinary people who, at certain points in their lives, learned to unfold ever-deepening levels of thought. And at least one example of the frustration that can occur when a person reaches the bottom of the pool once, only to never find his way back.

That particular tragedy, I am determined, will not befall you. To be certain of a successful conclusion to this, your initial journey to the bottom of the pool, we will use these pages as our primary vehicle. We will stop often, at virtually every point along the way.

As we edge ever deeper, I promise not to swim too fast. Instead, I will lead in a gradual manner, pointing out some of the often-ignored, but very important, points along the way.

One caution: stay alert at all times. Occasionally we will execute a detour, and you must not miss the turn. These small deviations in direction will allow you time to examine a particular danger or to fully understand a seemingly insignificant part of your journey.

Please know that an intimate understanding of the thought process being revealed to you will make the difference in whether or not you are able to return to the bottom of the pool by yourself, whenever the need for a trip arises.

Yes, I intend to uncover the secrets. And I will show you the way. But I cannot apply the lessons for you. Only *you* are in charge of you. How and when and in which direction you think is a choice you must make on your own. I am honored to be your guide, but never forget that you own every part of this expedition.

As an aside, we will momentarily engage in a quick practice session of exiting the surface of the pool. This will be done to give you a quick taste of what the larger journey will be like. Afterward, there are safety issues to discuss, a few concepts with which you must become familiar, a specific strategy to learn, and several simulated situations in which you will come to fully understand the procedures of implementation.

Before long, after a single successful guided visit to the bottom of the pool, you will be officially certified to guide your own family, friends, or coworkers to this one-of-a-kind destination.

Don't promise them anything yet, however. At this moment they are splashing happily on the surface, and life probably seems pretty good to them. So let them have their fun. Soon you'll be able to effectively explain just how much better things could actually get.

For now, however, it's probably best you put that out of your mind. Don't worry about them. They are fine. And in reality, your friends aren't so unusual anyway. In fact, right this moment, at every pool in the world, despite being aware that a swim to the bottom is available any time they wish, almost every person in every pool is bobbing happily on the surface. And why wouldn't they be? It is safer on the surface, and there is a lot more company.

You know, the surface of a pool is an apt metaphor for the way we have been conditioned to live our lives. We *are* surface dwellers. Again, why wouldn't we be? There are obvious results at the surface—results we can verify with methods we can emulate. These results are achieved again and again by men and women who, in facing life's questions, consistently found answers that were correct.

We gain consensus of opinions on the surface. Almost everyone is willing to talk on the surface. They will tell us how a thing is done and why another thing won't work. And believe it or not, by virtue of so much experience, born of trial and error, almost without exception, the conclusions these experts have come to, the facts they share with us and the rest of the world . . . are absolutely true.

Obviously, with so much good and true information available from so many experts—these people who are already experiencing success in the areas of life we consider important—it just makes sense to spend our time on the surface. And so, we do.

Hey, here's a thought: When you were a kid and your parents

took you to the pool, in order for the adults to continue acting like the calm, rational human beings they believed themselves to be, in what area of the pool did they require you to stay? In the shallow water, right? But even in the shallow water, they wanted you to stay on the surface.

What happened if you *didn't* stay on the surface? Well, everything was fine as long as you went down only a little bit. And for a little while. Five or six seconds underwater and nobody thought it was a big deal.

But do you remember what the adults did the first time you swam underwater from one side of the pool to the other? They stood up, didn't they? They came to the side of the pool, watched your every move, and didn't relax until you returned . . . to the surface.

Just so you know, it isn't just the lifetime of conditioning that makes us reluctant to leave the surface. The most powerful challenge we face in choosing to leave the surface is the surface itself! Look around. There are credible people everywhere, men and women with influence who have years of experience and visible results. In addition, the answers one finds at the surface are helpful, overwhelmingly true, and generously shared. In fact, life itself is usually great at the surface.

GREAT!

It's a word that describes the hopes and dreams of a generation. Used as a designation, it is applied to a certain level of achievement in almost every positive activity the world can imagine. He is a great player. They are great parents. She is a great student or doctor or engineer. They are a great team. We had a great financial year.

The word accurately conveys where society's movers and shakers want to go: from "good" to "great." *Great* is the precise target for which the vast majority of us aim.

But why settle for *great* when *best* is waiting for you in slightly deeper water? And why don't more people aim for *best*? Probably for the same reason Bob Beamon was never able to duplicate the jump that had propelled him into track and field immortality. It's no great secret that the multitudes of people at the top of the pool are a lot louder than the folks at the bottom.

But why settle for *great* when *best* is waiting for you in slightly deeper water?

The Greats who occupy all that space on the surface—all those people who talk with absolute certainty about "what is" and "what is not" and "what can be done" and "what cannot be done"—their voices often overwhelm the softer whispers of the Best from the bottom of the pool.

Oh . . . and just so you're not surprised, you need to know that, even today, when someone like you leaves the surface heading for deeper water . . . it makes everybody really, really nervous.

Five

CAN HE . . . OR WILL HE?

It is interesting that Bob Beamon never again matched the results of his legendary jump. It had captivated the world. Several times during the years following that day, Beamon returned to the same Mexico City stadium. There he competed during the same time of year, with temperatures the same as it had been the day he set the record.

Beamon's attempts to equal or surpass 29 feet, 2.5 inches in that stadium were made in the same light atmosphere as before—the city was still situated at 7,382 feet.

Knowing that track and field records are not official if "wind aided" by a breeze higher than two miles per hour, every jump Beamon took in that stadium during the rest of his career was made with the knowledge that he was facing wind speed and direction that was virtually identical to that of the day his miracle had taken place.

More than once he was even surrounded by the same competitors. He wore the same colors, even the same shoes. But his results never approached what he had done the day he had been urged to "give 'em two inches on the front . . . take two feet when you land."

Why?

Within a year, that question was effectively answered by experts filing their reports from pool surfaces around the world. It had become increasingly obvious, they said, that Bob Beamon had been kissed by fate the day he had jumped 29 feet, 2.5 inches. His otherworldly leap, for whatever reason, had simply been a gift from God, a singular event, akin to being the only person in the history of mankind to actually see and lay hands on a unicorn.

Beamon's performance, the surface thinkers assured everyone, had been lightning in a bottle, caught once for a single instant, before vanishing forever.

Forever? That's what they said. And because the conclusions those experts came to at that time were true—and still are—this is where reality gets very, very interesting.

It would seem that the specific question asked by the experts at that time was an easy one to answer. It's a question that, in one form or another, has existed in our collective, and quite public, pool since way before the afternoon of October 18, 1968.

The question was asked out loud . . . and loudly. Posed by the experts at the surface, it was simple and direct. "Can Beamon do it again?"

Curiously the answer (again courtesy of the experts at the surface) began to form almost immediately after Beamon failed at his first attempt to "do it again." With each subsequent "failure" and an eventual injury, the experts became more convinced (and more convincing) that their answer was correct.

Magazines and newspapers at the time reflected the certainty of the experts. Bob Beamon, no doubt, was at least aware of these articles and the verdict that was in about his future.

Knowing that the quality of one's answers is usually determined by the quality of one's questions, it is unfortunate that no one—at least, no one publicly—asked anything that might have given a young man participating in an individual sport the opportunity to come to a different conclusion about himself.

So more than a half century after the fact, why don't you and I examine some questions that were never asked . . .

1. If in the previous one hundred years the long jump record was broken only thirteen times by an average of two and one half inches, would it be reasonable to assume that no competitor in the history of the sport ever walked to the starting block thinking he might break the world record by two feet?
2. On October 18, 1968, as he stood in the starting block, did Bob Beamon consider breaking the world record by two feet? Well, according to what Ralph Boston said to

the twenty-two-year-old Beamon immediately before his jump—"Give 'em two inches on the front. You'll take two feet when you land"—we know the possibility of such a leap had at the very least been placed in his mind.

3. In your lifetime, have you experienced days when, for no particular reason, you felt physically stronger—you had more energy—than you felt the day before or the day after? *Were* you physically stronger? Did you actually have more energy? Assuming "greater strength and a higher energy level" are more productive than "less strength and a lower level of energy," at what point did you decide that the twenty-four hours following a great day would be "not as great"? Did you actually decide? Have you ever considered any *feeling* you have had to be the result of an active choice?
4. In your lifetime have you ever stepped on a scale feeling thinner and more fit only to find your weight was virtually the same as a few days before when you felt run down and overweight?
5. Does a mind have wings? When Ralph Boston told Bob Beamon that his legs had never been stronger, did Beamon believe him? When Boston declared that Beamon's body weighed nothing, what did Beamon think? When he heard "At this moment your body weighs nothing," *how* did Beamon think?
6. **Whether you think you can or think you can't . . . either way, you are correct.** Have you found this statement

applies in any way to the results you have experienced during your lifetime? Have you found it applies more accurately to other people than it does to you? On October 18, 1968, in the moment before his jump, was Bob Beamon thinking he could "take two feet"? In the moment before his jump, was there room in Beamon's head for the possibility that he could not?

7. Was Beamon's jump really "lightning in a bottle, caught once for a single instant, before vanishing forever"? When "Can Beamon do it again?" was first asked, was there anyone who recognized the damage being done by this horrible question?

Does a mind have wings? Absolutely. Unfortunately, a mind also possesses an anchor. And either can be deployed at the drop of a thought.

A mind with wings fully extended creates a flurry of appropriate action leading to positive results. These results are identifiable, even by casual observers who often describe what is happening as "momentum."

On the other hand, when a mind folds its wings and lowers its anchor, the diminishing results that occur are also identifiable, even by casual observers who often describe the negative situation as "a loss of momentum."

"Can Beamon do it again?" . . . Was there anyone who recognized the damage being done by this horrible question?

Is momentum important? Yes, if you're an athlete. Yes, if you're in business. Yes, if you intend to steer your family in a positive direction. Yes, in fact, if you have any kind of bandwagon and would like others to get on it!

The effects of momentum are easy to predict if one understands what its power actually does for a person. Incidentally, what momentum does for a person is exactly what it does for a team, a family, an organization, or a business. When one has momentum, the results of any action are greater than reality says they should be. Conversely, when one lacks momentum, the results of any action are less than reality says they should be.

In other words, with momentum, your team looks better than they really are. Without momentum, they look worse than they really are.

Is it possible that Bob Beamon actually lost momentum quickly after pulling off what is still considered the most stunning performance in track and field history? Yes, it's not only possible, it's exactly what happened.

How did it happen, you wonder? Let's go back to the horrible question, and as we think through it, I ask again that you be aware that the quality of one's answers is usually determined by the quality of one's questions.

Why then was "Can Beamon do it again?" the wrong question? For the shockingly simple reason that "no" was a horribly incorrect answer with devastating consequences. In fact, it was the trigger that released the anchor in Bob Beamon's mind.

If the question had been "*Will* Beamon do it again?" the answer "no" from any source would have been perfectly acceptable.

Because it would have been an opinion—a guess—with no more power to sway Beamon's mind than your average fairy tale.

But the question was "*Can* Beamon do it again?" And the answer to that should have been a resounding *yes!* Because he had already done it. Bob Beamon was obviously physically capable of leaping 29 feet, 2.5 inches. Obviously? Yes, because he actually did just that.

So if Beamon was physically capable of jumping that distance once, what was to stop him from doing it again? It couldn't have been a physical barrier. He had already proven to the world—and to himself—that his body was capable. Therefore, the only possible barrier was one created in his own mind.

On an October afternoon in 1968, there was a moment—in a stadium full of screaming people—that Bob Beamon listened to one voice. It was the voice of his mentor. Ralph Boston's words gave wings to Beamon's mind, and those wings propelled his body through the air to a mark well beyond what any other athlete had ever imagined.

Soon after his triumph in Mexico City, however, quite the opposite phenomenon took place. Instead of listening to the voice that told him what was possible, Beamon's mind was besieged by the voices of experts declaring that *what he had already done* . . . was impossible.

In effect, Bob Beamon's mind prompted his body to perform to its potential on one particular day when he was twenty-two years old. On every other day during the rest of his career, that very same mind told exactly the same body that the record jump—the jump the body had already done—was a freak of nature, a fluke, an outlier.

In essence, Bob Beamon told Bob Beamon that Bob Beamon would never be able to jump that far again.

And he never did.

PREFACE

I wonder: How often do *you* totally skip the preface to a book? Personally, my answer would be "very." And I'm not sure why that is. Perhaps my ADD is kicking up, and I just want to get to the main content. So, very often, I skip everything in a book before chapter 1.

Statistics about readers and their reading habits would show that if you, too, rarely read a preface, then you and I are among the majority. Once, I actually saw a statistical analysis on how *few* people read the preface to any book, and I was . . . what? Shocked? Stunned? No, I was *not surprised*.

Why? I suppose I was not surprised the percentage of non-preface-reading readers was so low because most of the prefaces I have read were boring and unnecessary.

That having been said, I *really* wanted you to read my preface. So I put it here. After chapter 5.

"Did your publisher approve this idea?" you might be asking.

No, of course not. You see, there is "a way these kinds of things are done." And this is not the way.

Neither does my publisher like it when I put more than one exclamation point at the end of a sentence. Excessive italics, bold type, and font changes shake book people up in a way missed deadlines never could. I am told that a defibrillator was installed in the hallway outside my publisher's office door. But I shouldn't brag.

And . . . they don't like a lot of these dots . . . (They call them "ellipses." You and I know them as dots.) And . . . they are less than thrilled when I start a phrase with the word *And* or *But*.

But . . . I do it ANYWAY!!!

My reasoning is fairly straightforward. I'm imagining a conversation with you as I write. I'm writing as I assume you and I would actually talk were we in the same room. I hear your questions. I understand your doubts. And occasionally, I feel your fear. Therefore, imagining that you can hear me, I see these pages as a barrier between us that I attempt to bridge by pausing with the dots . . . slowing my speech with italics, and turning up the volume with a few exclamation points.

It's the only way I can speak louder in print!!!

Before we move past this preface, do you wonder why I chose such an odd place to include these thoughts in this book? The answer is not complicated. As I confessed earlier, I have skipped more prefaces than I have actually read. I'm not even mentioning the pass I have often taken on introductions and forewords.

However, being aware that you and I are a lot alike—and knowing for sure that I would pay attention to a preface that had been put in a goofy place like this—I readily admit that my desired result was what has now occurred: that you read the preface.

Wait! Don't go away . . .

Yes, the preface you are reading at the moment *is* located in what appears to be a ridiculous location. And while I did position the preface here in order that you would read it, the fact that you actually *are* reading it allows me to reveal the primary reason I put it here in the first place.

In short, I wanted to present a "proof" in order to assure you that the time you are investing, the concentration it will require, and the swim you are about to take will be worthwhile. The truth you will discover at the bottom of the pool, should you choose to harness its unique power, will allow you the opportunity to create incredible outcomes from what would ordinarily be considered reasonably successful situations.

And this preface has been your first proof that thinking beyond traditional boundaries can yield extraordinary results. Did you catch it?

To understand how the proof worked, you and I will need to think to a deeper, more literal place than exists on the surface. Remember that the surface is what everyone sees. The surface contains the logic and information that everyone knows. But we are about to dip *below* the surface. This is only a first look. Nothing hard. Nothing scary—just a simple step beyond where most ever venture.

Contemplate the challenge presented to every author by the preface that author has written to a book he or she has poured months or years into. The author of every book with a preface very much wants every reader to read that preface. Otherwise, why would the author have taken the time to write it? Why would the author have included it in the book?

Unfortunately, as you already know, statistics show that a majority of readers simply do not read a preface, no matter what.

Strangely enough, however, by placing the preface in a location so unexpected—so much so that the reader might even suspect a big mistake has been made by someone—*that* preface is read beginning to end by virtually everyone who owns the book.

Compared to the percentage of book buyers who read the preface in an average book, the results of this odd gambit might appear to some as a roll of the dice or a one-in-a-million shot. Not so. The fact that the preface location was strategically planned and the results precisely predicted provide you and me the proof that there is great value in thinking our way to a deeper understanding than that available on the surface.

This is just one example we will examine—an example of achieving extraordinary results by "taking a left" even though industry standards demand a right turn.

A deeper, more intentional thought process will very often move beyond what is true and go all the way to the truth. More on this concept later, but for now, consider this fact:

While it is true *that publishers always place a preface at the beginning of a book,*
the truth *is that a preface can be located anywhere the author desires.*

I believe the fact that you are still here bodes well for our relationship. So, thanks for reading this far. I intend to document and explain what I have learned during the past several years in hopes that you will gain some life-changing understanding. In order for that to happen, I also know that the content in this book has to be compelling enough for you to hang in here and think through it.

Think through it? Yes. It's the only thing I can really help you do. After all, I am not familiar with the intricacies of your life. Do you have an important relationship that is experiencing rough waters? Does your professional life produce the financial heights you expected? Has your family drifted beyond your reach? Only you know for sure where a massive infusion of extraordinary results is most needed.

Perhaps this is a simple thought, but it is of critical importance to me that this book be interesting. As you read, there may be times you experience the narrative line undulating wildly. Don't be afraid. Just hold tight with one hand while the other is waving goodbye to "the way everybody else does it."

The fact that the preface location was strategically planned and the results precisely predicted provide you and me the proof that there is great value in thinking our way to a deeper understanding than that available on the surface.

Six

THINKING BEYOND WHAT IS TRUE

Centuries ago in Europe it was customary for a judge to place a specific hat on his head before sentencing criminals. Because the judge was often the wisest person around, judges were considered "great thinkers." After a while the hat a judge wore became known as "a thinking cap."

I don't suppose anyone really believed that a particular head cover provided wisdom or correct answers, but it wasn't long before people everywhere were using the term in what is still a familiar phrase.

As a kid, when my mother wanted me to focus, to mentally bear down and concentrate, she would encourage me, preparing me for what I was about to learn or for a problem I needed to solve.

Figuratively, Mom would maneuver me to the starting line, and just before I began to dig into whatever I was supposed to read or do or fix or understand, she would prompt my beginning. She'd say, "Are you ready? Good. Then put on your thinking cap and get started!"

Several years ago I began to carefully reexamine some of the things I'd been taught to believe were true. To my relief, most of those things *were* true. Unfortunately many of them were not the truth.

It was with that unsettling awareness that I began a cautious but determined search for whatever reality might lie beyond the boundaries established in the name of "best practices," "industry standards," or "the way things are done." Curiously, I did not find the answers I had hoped for by looking to the left or right. Neither an angled perspective nor a treetop view provided much help either.

Down.

It was the last place I thought to look, but the treasure was indeed there. Not halfway down. All the way down.

It might be helpful to understand that *in every profession, there is an average outcome.* Though personal averages are not discussed as often, there is also an average outcome in our private lives. As parents, spouses, or citizens of the community, each of us produces a result. Lumped together, our outcomes tallied and averaged, there is, by definition, an average—or ordinary—result. Most of those ordinary results are good, and some might even cross the threshold into the category termed *great.*

In this present endeavor, you and I are targeting a place well beyond that. As our journey progresses, it will be helpful to continue to consider this fact:

Any answer that is true will produce workable, occasionally excellent, results.

However, that is exactly why most people never seek a deeper understanding of the issue. It never occurs to them to do so! After all, they found the answer, the answer was true, and it produced the expected results.

In fact, the higher the achiever—the closer to the top of any field of endeavor one is acknowledged to be—because of the results they have already produced, the less likely they are to attempt thinking beyond what got them there in the first place.

There does exist, however, a deeper understanding of almost any subject you and I might consider important. That deeper understanding is available to all who seek it, for it lies within reach of any person who desires the wisdom it provides.

The most often accepted definition of wisdom is "a deeper understanding of principle." If one desires to do business or parent or compete in a principled

The higher the achiever—the closer to the top of any field of endeavor one is acknowledged to be—because of the results they have already produced, the less likely they are to attempt thinking beyond what got them there in the first place.

manner, doesn't it make sense that an understanding of whatever principle applies in a particular situation would be necessary? And wouldn't the value of the principle be more effective when the understanding of it increased to a level of *deeper* understanding? Further, is there a level of understanding that is greater than deeper? Yes. And, oddly enough, that level would be described as "deeper."

Wisdom's power is sometimes closer than we expect but is more often found embedded in the principle's foundation. It is deep down, found only on purpose, and contains the might to change the world if given a chance. Its reality exists well beyond all we know that is merely true.

We call this stalwart, unconquerable ally . . . *THE TRUTH.*

Seven

IMAGINING A SENSE OF HUMOR

Are you smiling? Right now, I mean . . . I'm assuming you have on your thinking cap? What does it look like? A bit silly perhaps?

Even if you weren't smiling before, how about now? Smiling? Just a little bit?

Excellent!

Hey, there's no one here but us. Is a quick break okay with you? I need to stretch for a couple of minutes, maybe do a little jogging in place. Oh, let's make sure our thinking caps are snug and secure too.

If you didn't notice my admiring glance, I must say that yours looks particularly fashionable on you. I like the way you wear it a bit low, cocked rakishly at that angle. No, I don't think the red is too much. And yes, it absolutely *is* acceptable to wear a thinking cap indoors.

Well, no, you wouldn't wear a *regular* cap indoors. Not the kind everyone can see, no. Definitely not. Not indoors. Did you know that the first time Alabama played in a domed stadium, Bear Bryant wouldn't wear his trademark houndstooth hat on the sidelines? He said it was because his mama told him a gentleman takes his hat off indoors!

But *this* is different. If you have yourself a good quality thinking cap, well, I've always figured that the more you wear it, the better off you'll be.

Several years ago, I had to add a chinstrap to mine. It works too. Maybe it was just me, but for a while there after I got it—and not always remembering to use it—every time I'd experience a stressful situation, my thinking cap would fall off or blow off. Naturally, I wouldn't even notice it was gone. And before you knew it, I'd made another questionable decision, one that I'd most likely never have come close to making if I'd had on my thinking cap.

That's why I got the strap. I just have to remember to buckle it.

Hey, before we get back to business, I'd like to say how much I appreciate you being willing to control your imagination and play along with the whole "thinking cap" thing! You've demonstrated a great sense of humor so far as well. Trust me, that's a plus.

It's sad to say, but I *do* occasionally cross paths with people who, no matter what, simply refuse to be a good member of a team unless they have been chosen as captain.

You know, regardless of how stressful or successful a momentary situation might be, a person's ability to outwardly demonstrate "enjoying the moment" as well as the ability to "be enjoyable to others in the moment" are critical, easily observable markers that reveal the stuff of which a person is made.

These markers indicate a person's degree of adaptability, patience, and current level of personal discipline. For those who build teams, it is important to weigh character virtues of this type before deciding the degree of responsibility with which a person can be entrusted.

Knowing that teams don't just play football—*families, corporations, and charitable organizations are teams as well*—a broadly developed sense of humor and the ability to control the expansion and limits of one's imagination can be hugely beneficial to everyone who is a part of the larger group.

Many times there are unspoken responsibilities a team member will quietly accept. There are unseen actions that a family member might perform consistently. In these acts of service, seemingly conducted under the radar, there is opportunity for constant and never-ending improvement to the attitude, work ethic, and results of everyone within reach. Anyone whose heart can be touched by kindness possesses a spirit able to comprehend another person's greater value.

Acquiring and employing a sense of humor is obviously a choice everyone makes for themselves, whether by design or default. The same is true of fueling one's present and future with a carefully controlled imagination.

If you have become mired in life's quicksand by default . . . if you *inadvertently* wandered down a pathway of negative results, there is wonderful news! Because you now know something that you didn't know only a moment ago! As quickly as you can snap the fingers of your mind, you can immediately begin to alter the trajectory of your future.

This reversal of destiny's fortune is more easily accomplished than you might suspect. And really, if you doubt that, aren't you only revealing *more* evidence that a different level of thinking might be in order? Seriously, don't you *want* the reversal of destiny's fortune to be easily accomplished? The answers—in case you are stumped—would be *YES* and *YES*.

Therefore, it is time to decide and act upon that decision immediately. Right now . . . flip the inner switch that activates your incredible sense of humor. If it has been dormant for some time, no worries. The pilot light has always been on. Wait for it . . . There! Did you hear that *whoosh*? Good. Me too. So, your sense of humor is on and anxious to be used.

Now, you can also begin to exercise the other personal gift we have mentioned—your controlled imagination!

In the Just So Ya Know category, though we are casually chatting through this subject during what you might be considering a quick break from the main point, don't think for a moment that I am kidding. In fact, I imagine myself to be pretty serious about the whole "sense of humor" thing.

And please don't be concerned that I seem to have strayed from the main point. I haven't. In reality, if you go too much further into this book without understanding the main point, you'll probably stop reading. Hmm . . . taking that into account, I suppose I should just make sure you understand the main point.

You.

The main point is you.

Look, read the chapters in order. Read them separately. Start the book in the middle if you want. It doesn't matter.

As long as you read with personal intent.

There are books you read to be entertained, books you read to be aware of advances made in your industry, and books you read seeking an understanding of opinion that opposes your own. When I encourage an attitude of personal intent, I am strongly suggesting you read this material having already specifically determined at least a few of your greatest hopes and dreams.

Keep in mind that most people never even bother to imagine what event or circumstance might need to occur in order to shift their life's results from acceptable to incredible. Instead, many of us—our minds flashing momentarily upon the possibility of incredible results—actively endeavor to control our imagination by shutting it down completely, never allowing ourselves to think about what might happen. Because we have already decided what will happen.

In other words, we can create an atmosphere in which we never recognize the many keys to greater results in every area of our lives that parade year after year directly under our noses. After all, how can anyone recognize a thing they have already convinced themselves does not exist?

Have you ever—or perhaps I should ask how many times—have you experienced something like this: you are in the kitchen and call to a family member, "Where is the coarse ground pepper?"

The answer comes back. "Over the sink with the spices."

You say, "I don't see it."

A bit exasperated, your family member asserts, "It's over the sink. I put it there less than an hour ago!"

Now you are a bit exasperated yourself. "Well, I'm telling you, I'm standing right here. I'm *looking* over the sink, and the pepper is not here!"

It is at that point your family member marches into the kitchen, nudges you aside, reaches above the sink to grab the coarse ground pepper, and holds it directly in your face.

Taking it sheepishly, you say, "Gosh, I'm sorry. I just didn't see it."

You're correct; you did not see the pepper. Of course you didn't see it. Standing right in front of the coarse ground pepper, you stated, "I don't see it." You said, "The pepper is not here!"

Your mouth tells your brain, "The pepper is not here." Your brain tells your eyes, "The pepper is not here." And as odd as it seems in the moment, your eyes do not see the pepper. It's all a function of imagination, of course.

And an imagination strong enough to make things disappear before your very eyes is also strong enough to see things that do not yet exist.

So . . . right now . . . imagine the previously unimaginable. What result do you consider beyond your abilities? Go there. Look at it from all angles. What specific answer do you need to make this dream a reality? Now, move forward, *reading with personal intent*. Imagine the answer you seek is hidden in this manuscript. And don't be surprised when you find it.

What the majority of people do, how they do it, and what happens when they do should not matter to you at this moment. Stop thinking about everyone else and what you think they might think about you or this book or anything else. Statistical anomalies are interesting but have no bearing on the main point.

The main point—*my* main point—is you.

You.

Neither of us is interested in the altogether too-common goal of *producing a bit more* than was achieved last time. No, no, no. I want to equip you to produce results far beyond those most people ever imagine. Or even imagine they *could* imagine! Then, I want you confidently capable of immediately turning around in order to double the results you produced before.

Right now, just remember that the main point is you; therefore, please control your imagination, harness it for your benefit, and shift your sense of humor into overdrive.

> **NOTE:** *Read the previous sentence again if you need to do so, but please be aware that though the tone of the instruction is lighthearted, this, your first exploration of the concept and subsequent*

journey to the bottom of the pool, will continue forward or fail quickly according to whether or not you take seriously the instruction above. So again, please, to be certain, reread the sentence that begins, "Right now . . ."

Got it? Excellent. Now that we have that agreement under our belts, I feel increased anticipation for our trip. After all, while I am prepared to play Meriwether Lewis to your William Clark, neither of us wants to blaze a trail through the Lemming Wilderness (otherwise known as "today's world") with a partner who lacks control over his imagination. Or doesn't have a sense of humor.

Our imaginations will do a great deal of the heavy lifting on this trip, directing us to pathways that—though they've always been in plain sight—have never been traveled.

By the way, do you wonder why I add the word *controlled* when referring to imagination? Because an *un*controlled imagination can create problems bigger than anything you want to face.

It is an unfortunate fact that people often allow themselves to become terrorized by their own imaginations. Fear. Rarely the product of reality, fear is nothing more than a misuse of the natural creativity we possess. Misusing our imaginations grants power to fear. Know that fear and its many demon relatives do not—and cannot—exist without a human host.

Even though the process by which fear and hate and rage take form is specific, these forces of destruction do not have the ability to spring into existence uninvited. They are never simply brought to life out of nothing. Instead, they are *thought* to life. By us.

That is correct. Are you remotely familiar with the wrecking ball of fear that, on occasion, blasts its way through your home, your family, and your business? While the damage done has been real, the wrecking ball, and the chain upon which it swings, only becomes a tangible threat when your imagination is allowed to roam without restraint.

Just remember that the main point is you; therefore, please control your imagination, harness it for your benefit, and shift your sense of humor into overdrive.

Unwarranted fear weakens a person's heart and spirit. Groundless fear ultimately produces uselessness from a heart and spirit—a heart and spirit that had been originally created as brave and powerful. Fear manifested and fed by an unbridled imagination will also greatly diminish the mental and emotional strength of family or team members and virtually anyone unfortunate enough to be nearby.

A person with an undisciplined imagination can spread fear like a plague, rendering the corporation or church or charitable organization completely demoralized by ordinary obstacles that suddenly seem to have morphed into the Mountains of Uncertainty.

Your imagination, however, from this moment forward, is under control.

It is under *your* control. The imagination owned and cared for by you is a consistent and reliable stream of chosen thoughts and ideas, each harnessed and directed . . . by you.

YOUR imagination, therefore, is a trusted source of ideas, undaunted by mirages of trouble and fear. When faced with mountains, your imagination can be depended upon to tunnel under or bore through, to fly over or drive across.

As for being able to laugh with others and laugh at oneself, that is also a bigger deal than most folks think. Therefore, please allow me to say again . . . I imagine myself to be pretty serious about the whole sense-of-humor thing. Wherever we are going and whenever we go, a great sense of humor will make everyone's trip a lot more fun!

Seven and a half

AND WHILE WE'RE ON THE SUBJECT . . .

. . . don't *EVEN* tell me you haven't got much imagination or that you don't have a very good sense of humor. If you really believe *that* about yourself, you might as well understand this too: You are living life in an unnecessarily tough way. And every day—by imagining you lack a funny bone—you're choosing to make it tougher still.

Knowing that you do *not* want to delay the implementation of all the stuff that is available to learn, be aware that it is perfectly acceptable to borrow a used imagination from a five-year-old child or a pre-owned sense of humor from one of your wittier friends.

Seriously, if you actually believe you don't have much

imagination or that you don't have a great sense of humor, please know that neither of those beliefs is true. Worse, they are lies. They are lies you have *told yourself.* But you need to understand that you did not come to those conclusions *by yourself.*

Most likely, you heard a snide remark about having no sense of humor from someone who wasn't as funny as they thought *they* were. Though the comment was made a long time ago, somehow it stuck. Now, without realizing you were actually buying into that belief through the years, you *have* changed. Because you were "smoked." Yep. Like meat.

If you've ever cooked with smoke, you know how tough it can be to get that smell off your hands. Even after multiple washings, the smoky odor will linger. But that's what smoke is supposed to do.

Curing meat is a slow process that allows the smoke to seep into every crack and crevice of whatever is being prepared. Smoke turns whatever you cook into a totally different food. Not sure about that? The taste is certainly different. Check your supermarket. You can buy ham. You can buy *smoked* ham. Turkey . . . or smoked turkey. Yeah, it's the same. Only different.

In a way, sometime in your distant past, you may have been "smoked" as well. You wouldn't be the only one to whom it's happened. For some reason it seems we occasionally put more credence in the opinions of other people about us . . . than we do in our own opinion of ourselves. It can happen. I know. I've done it myself.

But no more.

Allow me to clear this up for you. You have an awesome imagination and a great sense of humor. Don't argue the point. You can't. Anyway, do you want to believe the girl who said something stupid when you were in the eighth grade . . . or me?

You never liked her anyway. Go with the easy answer . . . me.

Eight

ISN'T IT OBVIOUS?

Would it surprise you to know that Kevin Perkins and I have remained close friends throughout the years? Yep, we still see each other often and connect in some way on a regular basis. Some time ago, Kevin and his wife, Glenda, were at our house for dinner. As usual, we were all telling stories and laughing uproariously.

Somehow the subject of "Summers When We Were Children" came up, which led to that topic's popular subcategory, "Swimming Pool Stories," and, before long, Kevin and I had accessed our mental drop-down menu and were regaling our boys with that bracket's gold-medal tale. As you might have already guessed, it is our classic account of "The Day the Dolphin King Was Dethroned."

Later, Kevin and I were pleased to hear our wives remark (without excessive sarcasm) how much it added to our presentation when we acted out the techniques we had used back then.

That evening, after Kevin and Glenda were gone, Polly was getting ready for bed, the boys were doing all the homework they had "forgotten" while Uncle Kevin was telling stories, and I was outside walking our dog, Carver.

Suddenly, after all the years that had passed and as many times as Kevin and I had told the tale of Dolphin, a new thought occurred to me.

As kids, we worked hard at improving our Dolphin skills. We grew physically, of course, but we also searched for a competitive edge. We practiced what we learned. We even visualized winning.

Meanwhile, as I mentioned earlier, Aaron already had a competitive edge and grew physically as well. Beyond that, however, he didn't attempt to improve. He didn't look for new techniques, and he certainly never practiced.

Thinking through everything that had happened that summer, still walking the dog, I came to another conclusion. I stopped and frowned, deciding that Aaron probably never visualized winning either. He didn't need to visualize winning, I realized. Because he always won. Heck, Aaron won every time!

Why would he have needed to learn anything else? From Aaron's perspective, what was there to learn? Why would he have needed to practice?

That night, outside in the dark with Carver, something else began to bug me, and I couldn't figure out what it was. It was the same feeling you get when a name won't come to you. It's on the tip of your tongue, the edge of your brain, but you just can't tie it down.

Everything I knew made perfect sense. I wasn't even sure why I continued to think about it. As I said, I already knew why Aaron hadn't practiced or ever attempted to learn anything new. What was there to learn? He was the already the best.

Think carefully here as we repeat a thought from chapter 1. It's the same thought that felt so weirdly incomplete that evening after Kevin and Glenda had left.

> **Azalea Pool was the only place in the world the game of Dolphin was being played. We were the kids who had invented the game. We were the game's best players in the world because we were the *only* players in the world. That meant, of course, that Aaron Perry was the best Dolphin player . . . *in the world*.**

That evening, as sometimes happens in my life, while Carver was on a leash, my mind was not. Yes, I stayed with the dog, but I sent my imagination in a different direction. And I did this on purpose. Continuing my walk, I decided to imagine my childhood in a different way—this time with the game we had invented having become as popular as baseball and football.

In my imagination Dolphin had caught on, spreading all around the world. In America, regional leagues were covered by local news, and the Professional Dolphin Association (the PDA) held their matches on national television.

Fantasy Dolphin had become an obsession for many, and

online teams in office buildings around the world formed leagues of their own. The Fantasy Dolphin concept had been created, owned, and managed by the same fine folk who had brought us professional wrestling years before.

> We also searched for a competitive edge. We practiced what we learned. We even visualized winning.

To those who considered themselves Dolphin purists, Fantasy Dolphin seemed ridiculous. Most did, however, appreciate the irony of a game called Dolphin that was created by kids in a swimming pool that had now morphed into office pools for Dolphin—an activity creating billions of dollars—though no one actually went near the water!

The most amazing Dolphin fact, however, was that despite participation from hundreds of thousands of athletes the world over, Aaron Perry was still unbeaten.

Suddenly, I stopped walking. I just stopped.

ALERT!

The next eight paragraphs are a detour. As the reader in charge, you are free to use the detour as a short break from serious thought. If you'd rather not spend the roughly ninety seconds that will be consumed by traveling this route, feel free to skirt the following eight paragraphs completely and continue on the main road as if this detour did not exist.

* * *

Occasionally, the expression emanating from the essence of me, myself, and I (all three of us!) will cause my wife to lift her eyebrows and wave a hand in front of my face.

She seems to think I have blanked out. I have not and am merely taking a moment to confirm a suspected connection. Nevertheless, my wife continues to believe that I have somehow become unconscious while still able to function.

I insist that I am merely "going away for a moment" to grab pieces of a few things that perhaps might be useful in some way if combined. After all, I maintain, how many centuries passed before Mr. Reese came into work with chocolate in one hand and peanut butter in the other?

In response to the eye-rolling and laughter of my wife, I usually have nothing to claim except a "this is how I work" and offer as evidence the twenty-something books with my name on their covers.

Upon hearing my best explanation for the frequent out-of-body experiences my mind initiates, my lovely wife often says absolutely nothing in response, choosing instead to display her sweetest (and most infuriating) smile. In my heart of hearts, however, I will admit that the evidence she is able to present supporting her argument is crushing. I suppose I could write a thousand books and still not be able to explain why, yes, occasionally, I do drive past my own driveway.

In addition: yes, I really have gotten off the interstate for gas, returned to the interstate after filling up, and driven seventy miles back the same way I had come before noticing anything was amiss.

Yes, it is curious that I make my living *noticing* things for companies and teams, have written a *New York Times* best-seller titled *The Noticer,* and once actually walked in and out of our living room for a whole week *without* noticing the furniture had been rearranged. Yes, I realized it then only because my wife pointed it out.

In my defense, while it may appear to some that I am blanking out, I insist that in those moments, I am merely working in an alternate location. I think of these times as if I'm searching for an answer to a question that no one has yet asked. Having finally grasped the frayed ends of several different-colored wires, I know I have everything I need for a breakthrough. Touching this wire to that one or those two to another, soon we will light up the darkness. But, first, we must confirm a connection!

ALERT!

Readers merging onto main road below.

Carver tugged at the leash in my hand, and I realized I had been standing still for . . . well, I didn't know for how long. As I began walking again, my first conscious thought was, *Okay . . . Aaron is* still *the best in the world.*

I began to engage with how I imagined my new reality would have unfolded. In that situation, I reasoned, with the game being played across the world, the participants would undoubtedly cover the gamut in terms of skill levels. There would be great players, good players, average players, poor players, and beginners.

Even though worldwide interest would have created a large group of great players, only Aaron remained undefeated. Obviously playing the game at a different level, Aaron Perry was one of a kind, acknowledged as the greatest of them all.

I mused that if the game had popularized to *that* degree, there would be clinics and classes dedicated to coaching Dolphin techniques. Probably books on the subject. Online courses.

And finally, this: If several of the world's greatest Dolphin players held a clinic in Aaron Perry's hometown, he would probably not even attend. Why not? Because he was the best. And since he was the best, what could anyone possibly teach him?

No one knew more about the game of Dolphin than Aaron Perry. He held every record in the sport. Aaron had better results than anyone. Anyone ever. Ever! Therefore, the evidence of his superiority was undisputed. And it wasn't just Aaron who thought that. *Everyone* understood—they believed—they *knew* . . . that there was nothing more the man could learn. Aaron knew it all. That was obvious.

At least, it was obvious until Kevin Perkins went *down* instead of up.

For at that point:

Everything that had been so obvious . . .was no longer even true.

Nine

WELL . . . *THAT* CHANGES EVERYTHING

I must admit that it was a long time before I even started to connect these dots that seemed to flit just out of my reach, but slowly, and very quietly at first, an alert began to sound in my head. *Wake up*, it seemed to say.

The alarm was not constant. Neither did it get very loud. But because it was unpredictable—going off at any time of the day or night—the alarm certainly was unnerving. Finally, with more of a soft realization than a lightning flash of brilliance, I understood something about that childhood game that had an odd bearing on my adult life.

At that time, as children competing in a simple game, each

one of us believed that we were doing the best we could do; we believed ourselves to be performing to the best of our abilities.

Because we knew how the game was played—treading water in the deep end of the pool—and because we knew our physical limitations, there was another significant belief in play. In addition to believing that each individual was doing the best he or she could do, we firmly believed that each individual was doing *the best that could be done.*

HOWEVER . . .

While we *were* doing the best we could do, we were *not* doing the best that could be done.

In reality the Best That Could Be Done would never—*could* not ever—occur until a player got to the bottom of the pool.

You see, in the game of Dolphin, a player can kick his feet, stretch out, and flail hands and arms as much, as hard, as fast, and as efficiently as he is able. The player can perform these moves from the surface, from eighteen inches under the surface, or from any mid depth he chooses. But the reality is that *until he reaches the bottom of the pool, he will never realize his true potential.*

In the game of Dolphin only the bottom of the pool can produce the "best that could be done." For, in any pool, only the bottom of it can provide a foundation solid enough to push against, allowing the player the opportunity to harness every ounce of power available.

Dolphin has much in common with life as we live it. If you and I were to ask an ordinary person, "Are you doing the best you can do?" the likely answer from that person would be, "Yes, I am." And that answer would probably be true.

Suppose then we followed up with this: "Are you doing the best that could be done?"

Most likely, the answer would come in the form of a confused expression on the person's face. Why?

Because most people who are doing the best
they can do
(especially if they are among the best at *what*
they do)
are not often remotely aware
that a significant amount of territory still exists
beyond that which they have already achieved!

Whether we call you a businessperson, a parent, or any of a thousand other ways society labels who you are or what you do, there is a description available and widely used for the actions you perform on a daily basis. Whatever that might be, it constitutes an extremely important part of your life.

How well you do, how much you produce, how valuable you become, how far you go, how high you climb . . . each of these concepts of measure are familiar to us and are regularly considered by us. Exactly where on that admittedly arbitrary scale of accomplishment other people believe us to be directly affects our families' quality of life. Because how skilled or how important or how rare other people believe we are is the major factor in the influence we are granted and the income we are allowed to earn.

Because most people who are doing the best they can do (especially if they are among the best at *what* they do) are not often remotely aware that a significant amount of territory still exists beyond that which they have already achieved!

Though most of us are judged (by ourselves and others) to be performing to the best of our ability, in reality, the results of our efforts are invisibly restricted by three things:

1. What we know about the most accomplished people—living or dead—who have ever done what we want to do. And the best results *they* ever achieved.
2. What we understand about *how* it is traditionally done.
3. Where we believe our own abilities measure up to the first two considerations.

So. Are you and I doing the best we can do? Yes.
That is true.
But are we doing the best that can be done? No.
Not even close.
And that . . . is the truth.

Ten

IMAGINING BEYOND IMAGINATION

Here's an odd fact known by few: Walt Disney was eighteen years old when he was fired from his first job as a cartoonist for the *Kansas City Star* newspaper. The reason? According to his boss, Walt "lacked imagination and had no good ideas!"

Knowing how everything turned out, it's strange enough that Disney was dismissed in the first place, but that he was fired for a lack of imagination and bad ideas is almost inconceivable, isn't it?

It is a good thing Walt didn't allow an opinion to direct his life. Let me tell you what no one saw at the time . . . or if anyone *did*, he didn't have the guts to say anything about it. It was not

Walt Disney who lacked imagination. It was his boss. It was Walt's boss who lacked the imagination to recognize the incredible talent walking through the office door every day.

Think about it: Where Disney worked, having a good imagination was a key part of the job. Yet the boss fired Walt for work he determined was lacking in imagination.

In the boss's defense, he was clueless. He was clueless about the level of talent right in front of him. Walt Disney obviously had an imagination, but, to the boss, it was unrecognizable. Why? Because Walt didn't merely have a few percentage points *more* imagination than the ordinary guy. If that had been the case—a little more, a little less—the boss would have identified it.

Instead, Walt had *so much more* imagination than anyone the boss had ever encountered, Disney probably seemed to be from another planet! Of course, we know now that wherever Walt *was* from, he would one day reside in a Magic Kingdom!

Since all we know for sure is that Disney was fired for "a lack of imagination," it is somewhat ironic that you and I will need to use our own imagination to find our way to the bottom of the pool about this. Something happened back then (it was 1919) that was true. It appears, however, that a lot of people missed the truth. Certainly about Walt Disney, anyway!

To begin, I'm guessing no one called the young man into an office and said, "You're fired. You lack imagination. Your ideas are horrible."

More likely, it happened something like this:

"Walt . . . come in. Have a seat, son. Listen . . . I have some tough news to deliver here. This is not easy for either of us, but I will say first that I'd like to make this as constructive for you as I can.

"I do want to say that we here at the *Kansas City Star* have appreciated your efforts. As sorry as I am, you and I both know that efforts alone are not enough, at least not in this industry. In cartooning, Mr. Disney, Kansas City is the big leagues. We gave it a shot. It just didn't work out.

"As hard as it is to hear, we at the *Star* are letting you go. Again, I am sorry, but the constructive piece for you, I believe, is that at your age, a complete change of scenery is easier to accomplish than it would be for someone older.

"By a complete change of scenery, I mean to suggest you move in a different direction—perhaps a different industry altogether. We . . . and by 'we' I am referring to your supervisors and myself here at the *Star* . . . we just don't feel you've been able to get a good grasp on how things are done in this industry. Specifically, your work—while again, your efforts were admirable—it was . . . off base.

"In short, we simply believe you lack the imagination or the ideas required for success here. I wish you nothing but the best in the future."

Wow.

Can you imagine someone calling Walt Disney into the big office and telling him that

a. his efforts were appreciated (attempting to *nicely* deliver a falling ax),
b. he didn't have a grasp on how things were done in that industry (explaining how far off base his work seemed to everyone in the company), and
c. he was lacking imagination and good ideas?

I can't either. For now, though, put aside A and C.

As for A, Disney probably didn't hear it. He was being fired. If he did hear it, he didn't believe it. Good for him. And you and I know now that C was just flat out wrong, incorrect, or however else you'd like to characterize one of the worst business decisions in history.

B, however, is very interesting. In today's world it is this line of thinking that is consistently used to justify saying no to a fresh idea or avoiding the possibility of a different direction. When a declaration like "This is the way it's done" is made, it is evidence of *someone* instructing *everyone* to tread water. References to "industry standards" or "best practices" are much the same.

This type of thinking is not bad. In fact, it does not spell disaster for an organization. It is merely the default position. This is the traditional mind-set of most organizations that society considers successful. Not extraordinarily successful. Just successful.

In other words, the leader who distributes the book of best practices, gives away framed copies of industry standards, and has the staff pledge allegiance to "the way things are done" has tied extra-large life jackets on everybody. Yeah, your motto might as well be "safety first" because none of your people will get anywhere close to the bottom of the pool.

For a quick moment, look back at B.

The company had decided that Walt didn't have a grasp on how things were done in the industry. They said he was far off base. Far? Yep. If we consider "base" to be the industry standard . . . or "normal" . . . then in the boss's opinion (which mirrored the industry's opinion), Walt Disney was either too far away from normal in one direction . . . or too far away in the other.

When a declaration like "this is the way it's done" is made, it is evidence of *someone* instructing *everyone* to tread water.

Which means . . .

The company either decided that Disney was overly dull and behind the times . . . or they thought he was absolutely whacked out! To his contemporaries, Walt Disney was considered too crazy to be taken seriously.

Can't you just hear it?

"Walt! Come on, man . . . what? A talking mouse? Really?"

Okay, stop laughing. I mean, it *is* funny, but here's an odd thought: What the boss told Walt—that he wasn't producing work that fell within the industry standard—was true. The problem seems to be that the boss didn't know there was anything *beyond* what was true. After all, the *desired* industry outcome was to produce steady results.

Of course, we now know that it wasn't only Walt Disney (and the mouse he had drawn on a napkin) who had been banished from the *Kansas City Star*. The boss and his newspaper's avoidance to thinking beyond the industry standard ensured their future would never include a duck named Donald, a dog we call Goofy, or the beautiful girl who—to this very day—lives in a forest with seven dwarves.

Make no mistake, however—the boss's mission was accomplished. The shareholders never knew the eighteen-year-old had been fired because they never knew he existed. If the *Star*'s board of directors were aware of Walt, they never questioned the dismissal because nothing appeared to have been lost. The boss certainly had no second thoughts.

On the other hand, by firing Walt Disney, the boss shut the door on any possibility of astonishing results that might have occurred in Kansas City (Meet Cinderella tonight at Arrowhead Stadium!), opting instead to protect the company's ability to continue producing *ordinary* results—the industry standard kind—the kind that allowed the boss to keep his own job.

Seen from a distance like this, the whole thing is mighty curious, isn't it? Speculation? Some of it, perhaps, but I feel confident that what you and I just reconstructed was the truth. Can you feel it? Anytime you go as deep as you are able, even with your eyes closed, you'll know when you've made it to the bottom of the pool.

Walt Disney's mind allowed him access to deeper water. In other words, his imagination gave him the ability to think beyond the industry standards of the day. Just like you can think beyond the industry standards of tomorrow.

Here's a curious question: Do you think Walt forgot what

happened in Kansas City? Not that he was bitter . . . just . . . do you think he forgot? I don't. I'm sure that as a young man, Walt Disney had so many hopes and dreams as he walked into that newspaper building on his first day.

Think about it. He was a cartoonist at the *Star*. How many times during his boyhood had he wished for this? That first day, I wonder if he already had Jiminy Cricket in his head? If so, with Walt as happy as he must've been that first day on the job, did the young man already have a song in mind for the cricket in a top hat? Certainly he must have been

Wishing on the *Kansas City Star* . . .

Don't frown. It might have been sad then, but it's certainly not now! You already know how the story turns out. The end in Kansas City was the beginning of everything else. Being fired was the best thing that ever happened to Walt Disney . . . and it wasn't too much longer before he—and everyone else in the world—knew it.

Eleven

THE SECRET BENCHMARK

My wife and boys are *the* priority in my life. I write. And I speak. My schedule is pretty darn full as it is. Until recently, most people never knew that I would occasionally accept a corporate client on a yearly basis. I never talked about it from stage or during an interview. Neither did I advertise for clients—on my website or in any other format.

Today, while onstage or in an interview I might tell a story that refers to a client, I still do not advertise that I am available for an advisor/client relationship. Why? Because, *still*, for the most part, I am not.

Within reason, I am open to speaking for most corporations,

associations, and organizations. I enjoy the experience. But before I'll allow myself to seriously consider working with someone for an extended length of time, there are three specific criteria that must be met:

1. The new relationship and the time required must fit into my family life.
2. I gotta like 'em. Life is too short to be working with difficult or dull people—especially for a whole year—and I have learned that there is no amount of money that is worth a year of my life.
3. The Secret Benchmark.

My personal mission statement is this: "To help people live the lives they would live if they only knew how to do it." Because that is my purpose, I have no time to waste.

So as I talk with an organization's leader and work to decide whether a coaching relationship is a fit, I attempt to assess whether or not that person is truly seeking wisdom at this point in his life.

Does he or she demonstrate the ability to listen to someone else in order to learn?

Might I be one of those people?

Does this leader even know that there *is* anything else to learn?

Is this person open-minded?

How open-minded?

Does this person display an active imagination and likeable sense of humor?

Can this person think beyond the best that has already been accomplished? How far beyond?

Is this person willing to move past what is true in order to discover the truth?

But the final measure I must make—the Secret Benchmark that determines whether or not I can be of service to this leader or group of leaders—is this:

Will they go with me to the bottom of the pool?

Twelve

YOUR SPECIAL PLACE

In addition to all the time I spent at the pool when I was a kid, there was often opportunity to venture into the woods behind our house. In that vast, never-explored forest (three uncleared vacant lots), I built several forts.

Fort construction was simple enough—dig a big hole and drag an old piece of plywood across the top—and while these woodland palaces were not waterproof or even water resistant, they were incredibly effective protection from dangerous animals. They must have been, for though I maintained a keen eye, not a single lion or bear was ever spotted.

I enjoyed my forts and kept at least a couple of them provisioned at all times. Just the presence of candy and soft drinks does a lot to ease one's mind about the possibility of an emergency or unexpected company.

No emergency of any kind ever occurred, but visitors—once my fort locations became known—were a constant challenge to the ability I had developed of sneaking edible sustenance out of my mother's kitchen, across the back fence, and into uncivilized territory.

From those who called themselves my friends—Kevin, Danny, Bob, and the Luker boys to name a few—the only thanks I ever received were their frequent dares that I "do it again."

This constant pressure from my sugar-addicted buddies was the very reason I built a treehouse and never told a soul about it. Not easily seen from the ground, it was not so much a tree*house* as it was a platform of boards nailed between branches of a live oak. Fifteen or so feet into the air, I thought of it as my Perch of Solitude.

The forts were for playing army or entertaining guests, but the Perch was my private retreat. It was where I did my very best thinking.

Eventually, my family moved to another town. I was older, there was no jungle nearby, and I never built another treehouse. But I did learn to visit the old one in my mind. I found that it was possible to take a walk in our new backyard or find a quiet place in the house, close my eyes, and for a moment, sometimes even two or three, simply be still.

I began to see that wherever I was and whenever I needed to, it was possible to create a place of quiet, of deep thought, of greater understanding, of higher connection.

The original Sherlock Holmes called this place his "brain attic." More contemporary versions of Holmes have upgraded it to a "mind palace." For Sherlock, this was a place where he cataloged experiences of the past and drew upon them to sort out the great mysteries of his present. I'm asking you to go a step further. Put that fine imagination to work sometime very soon and create your own Location of Contemplation. Obviously, it doesn't have to be a physical place. After all, what if you're out of town when you need it?

So, first and foremost, dust out an unused corner of your mind. Take a deep breath, close your eyes, and begin. Choose the location. Create its view and colors. Decorate it however you wish.

This is a place that will be available at any moment and always, only for you. You don't have to use the place on any schedule or for any set amount of time. Its availability, along with the quiet peace you'll choose to create there, is what will eventually produce a unique ability in you.

You will be able to move from the surface to the bottom of the pool and back. You will make the trip at will, without risk, and with any subject in tow.

Consistent, extraordinary results—like the ones that exist in your future—are created on purpose.

Knowing you wish to create extraordinary results, please understand that you'll need to think in an extraordinary direction. Know that it is possible for anyone to win the lottery once. But consistent, extraordinary results—like the ones that exist in your future—are created on purpose. Step one, of course, is learning how to leave the surface and not immediately pop right back up!

That's why you are creating your new space—your very own Location of Contemplation. Trust me, you will find many additional uses for it. You'll enjoy your time there. At first, however, the primary use of your special place will be to learn how to enter, sit down, and stay inside for at least ninety seconds. Incredibly, that small amount of time is often enough to explore a possibility that everyone around you is ignoring.

Concentrate your thoughts into the contrary direction.

The bottom of the pool is the ultimate in a "contrary direction," but it is the only place you can consistently find answers that are contrary to the answers that have become the industry standard, those that have produced ordinary results for years.

Thirteen

BEYOND THE BOX. PLEASE!

Beyond is a good word for us at the moment, though in a number of years, I'm certain we will need another word—another one that means something beyond *beyond*.

A decade or so from now, you and I will be somewhere together hearing a concept explained. There will be a word or a phrase spoken that will cause us to slowly turn toward each other. Our eyebrows will rise and both of us will know that the world is catching up.

No worries. Not now or then. Hit the gas and let's go. Where? I'm not certain at the moment. I do know, however, that wherever everyone else finds themselves at the time, you and I will be headed beyond.

By the way, with apologies to every person in the world who used the phrase *outside the box* ten times yesterday, can you and I move past that one? Allow me at least the opportunity to point out that if you have become married to the concept of being "outside the box," you should recognize the reality that you ain't outside it anymore.

As a Professional Noticer, I've observed an odd trend during the past several years. It is that virtually everywhere I go people pride themselves on thinking outside the box. The phrase, the concept, the impromptu speech about it is in use everywhere. By everyone. Corporations, small businesses, organizations, associations, teams, churches, communities, neighborhoods, even families. Everybody is thinking outside the box!

And if *everyone* really is outside the box, doesn't that mean we have arrived at a point in time where *no one* is actually outside the box?

Quickly now . . . into your Location of Contemplation! Settled? Excellent.

The phrase *outside the box* is used to describe thinking *differently* or thinking *a bit ahead of the competition*, correct? That being true, it *is* an advantage if you or your company are a part of the 5 percent thinking outside the box.

As part of the elite 5 percent, your results are stratospheric compared to those of the 95 percent, and you are thrilled, giggling softly on the phone, shushing each other in the hallways. Because you know something *they* don't know.

Until they do.

As more and more people begin to crowd the hallway outside the box, their results become more similar to those of the initial 5 percent. And in an odd form of hero worship, most of us continue to honor or follow or be intimidated by that company or team who was first out of the box. We never seem to realize that we are standing right beside them. And we have come to accept that *what we all do* is how it is done.

And if *everyone* really is outside the box, doesn't that mean we have arrived at a point in time where *no one* is actually outside the box?

In college football there are various rule changes from year to year, and occasionally a superstar athlete will show up. These shifts can appear to give one team or another a brief advantage. During its more than one-hundred-year history, though, college football changes slowly.

Sure, there will be new offensive wrinkles or different defensive schemes from the year before, but for the most part, we, the fans, see what we are used to seeing. And we like it. The industry standard has held up well.

Consider for a moment the time used between plays. That "empty time" begins when a whistle is blown by an official signifying the end of a play. The players get up off the ground, stretch or catch their breath, and move toward the line of scrimmage. Meanwhile, the coaches on the sidelines send in a substitute or two, and the players they are being subbed for run off the field.

At that moment, history tells us that there are eleven players on the field. Traditionally they come together and hold a short meeting—called a huddle—about what their next play will be, before moving to the line of scrimmage.

Looking over his offense, the quarterback takes a few seconds to step to the line, checking out the defensive formation across from him. Moving under center, the quarterback barks signals to his offense, confirming or changing what they had decided in the huddle, and the ball is snapped. A new play begins.

For decades this process between plays took an average time of thirty-two seconds. Then, in 2007, the Oregon Ducks hired Chip Kelly as their offensive coordinator. In 2009, Kelly was named head coach. By 2010, the Ducks had done away with huddles entirely. They created a way to communicate plays from the sideline using signs, virtually eliminated substitutions during a drive, and cut the time in between plays to 23.2 seconds.

The 23.2 seconds, versus the 32 seconds everyone else was used to, meant the Ducks were moving the game along at a pace that was 32 percent faster than their opponents had prepared to play. And 23.2 was just the average. There were drives during that 2010 season in which the Ducks used only 9.9 seconds between plays.

Opposing teams were stunned and confused. In the history of college football, if a coach ever tried anything different, it was usually something to slow the game down . . . to give the players time to catch their breath.

But this?

Kelly's offense was creating situations where the opponents faked injuries just to stop the game for their teams before anyone had a heart attack! The Oregon home crowd booed the officials who couldn't move the chains fast enough to keep up with Duck first downs. Seriously!

What Chip Kelly had done was absolutely within the rules, but it was clear to everyone that the Ducks were outside the box. Wow! Yes, they absolutely were outside the box.

And now . . . they're not.

Kelly led the Ducks to a BCS National Championship Game before being lured to the NFL. By that time there were many college programs running the same offense, and whether they did or not, the defenses were no longer surprised. In the six years since Kelly left, the Ducks have now hired their *third* head coach. They switched their offensive scheme to a "spread" in 2015 and switched again to a "pistol" formation in 2018.

As for you there in your personal Location of Contemplation, I'd like for you to think *beyond*.

In 1960, when Walt Disney hired Mike Vance to become dean of the newly formed Disney University, it was Mike who popularized the phrase *thinking outside the box*. Before he passed away in 2013, Vance had been a guiding force not only for Disney but also for others, such as Frank Lloyd Wright, Buckminster Fuller, and Steve Jobs.

Mike Vance accomplished things and helped people in a way a guy like me can only dream about. But with all due respect to Mike and everything he did, I have to think that job is done.

Honestly, is there anyone who isn't familiar with the phrase? Is there anyone who doesn't use it? So if we have reached a time in societal history where everyone is thinking outside the box, doesn't that really mean that no one, anymore, is "outside the box"?

It's time to think beyond the box.

Beyond. Not *around* the box. BEYOND.

There is a difference between thinking beyond outside the box and thinking around it. In any area that success is studiously observed, the greatest levels of achievement were almost always created by someone thinking outside the box. Naturally, achieving greater results with the least amount of wasted effort would necessitate beginning at that very point of greatest success. It was the culmination of a thrilling accomplishment for them. It is the starting line for you.

Consider that point of greatest success to be the end of the trail. In order to go beyond, you must clear additional brush; you must blaze more trail. To save time and energy, you would obviously use the end point of the previous successful trail as your beginning.

On the other hand, when a person thinks AROUND the outside of the box, they start by heading in a different direction entirely. Forced to blaze their own trail from the beginning, they are hoping to find something true and become successful in the same way they have seen others do.

Why not make use of what others have already determined to be true? Begin there. You are searching for the truth. Even on a trail, you can determine when you've reached the bottom of the pool.

Where others might have found what is true, they have also most often stopped there. Believing they have found "the answer," they announce the end of the trail and never attempt to go further. That . . . is the exact location you should choose to begin your quest. From that point, you think—and move—BEYOND.

So where do you and I want to be? BEYOND the outside of the box. Where is that? It is waaay out of town. Way out of what town?

Way out of the town in which there is an industrial complex
that has a street
upon which a building
is housing the very factory
that's manufacturing the boxes
that everyone else is sitting outside of.

Let everybody else think outside the box. You and I will think beyond it. Way beyond it.

We will think to infinity . . . and beyond!

Fourteen

HOW COULD I HAVE MISSED IT?

Several times each week, my family prepares lunch or dinner in the fresh, open air of our back porch. Pizza, vegetables, bread, meats—summer and winter—we cook entire meals outside.

Now, as you are imagining how we do this, do not imagine a gas grill. I gave mine away a long time ago. I still remember when I decided to get rid of it. My boys and I were on the deck. I was about to turn the knob to ignite the propane when Adam, the youngest of my sons, asked, "Can I do it? Please? It works just likc the stove inside . . ."

Adam didn't touch the knob, of course. I was standing right there, and despite his age, he knew this was a situation that required permission. It wasn't given. But just like that, I went to the bottom of the pool. I had been propelled by the words of a child.

I was there for only a few seconds and, at the time, did not describe it like that. Honestly, it was years before I would understand the process that had occurred. All I knew at the moment was that I would soon be giving away my previously treasured gas grill. Though millions of people were happily cooking outdoors on gas grills—doing the same thing as everyone else in the same way everyone else was doing it—I had just done a mental 180 and was already thinking rapidly in the opposite direction.

A single question from a little kid had cascaded into a series of thoughts, ensuring that from that day forward, given a choice, I would never use a gas grill again.

Curious, isn't it?

Do you remember watching your mom or dad stack a pyramid of charcoal and drench it in chemical fluid before standing back to flip a lighted match into the gathered vapor? *Whoomp!* Yeah, Daddy lost his eyebrows, but we're having burgers tonight!

After all the hassle we watched our parents endure just to cook a chicken or some steaks outdoors, when the gas grill was introduced, it almost seemed a miracle. Quite literally, millions of us thought in the same direction, and before long, most of our families boasted a gas grill on the backyard patio or deck.

I never mentioned it, but to me, the steaks or ribs or fish I grilled . . . well, none of it ever tasted like the food I remembered from my childhood. I was quietly ashamed that my efforts never approached the culinary perfection my dad reliably achieved with that rusted-out, wobbly, three-legged fire hazard he called a grill.

"Please, Daddy! Pleeeease, let me turn the knob!" Yes, that was the essence of the message Adam was attempting to deliver. All I really heard, however, was the declaration he made that the grill "works just like the stove inside."

Well of course it did! The stove in our kitchen started with the turn of a knob. So did the gas grill. When the knob on the stove was turned, the igniter sounded out with a *click, click, click, click* before the flame appeared with a gentle *poof*. So did the gas grill.

Raw at first, food prepared on the stove is exposed to heat of a certain temperature for a certain amount of time until it is considered "done."

Just . . . like . . . the . . . gas . . . grill.

Heat from the burner on a stove *only* cooks an item. Heat from the burner on a stove doesn't actually add any taste. The heat from the burner on a gas grill doesn't add any taste either.

The truth—the very reason for years of outdoor culinary disappointment—hit me like a ton of briquettes. No matter what I did, I was *never* going to match the taste of my father's grilled food. In reality, I might as well have cooked the steaks inside to begin with. They'd have tasted exactly the same.

Wait . . . before we move on, do you wonder why I took the time to tell this story? After all, it's not a tale of obtaining vast amounts of money or finding the long-sought cure for some dreaded disease.

The reason I include this chapter is because what actually

happened, and the process by which it occurred, is a much simpler example (than you might consider on your own) of the very thing you and I seek in every part of our lives. Results beyond the ordinary are available to you in every category of life. Professionally and personally, with all you care about, big things and small.

Never forget that for every part of your public and private existence, there is a level of understanding that will allow you access to results we would deem THE BEST. And always know that THE BEST results are far beyond the regular old "great results" with which everyone else has become satisfied.

And always know that THE BEST results are far beyond the regular old "great results" with which everyone else has become satisfied.

So these days, several times a week, I grab the big sack of natural charcoal and shake a few pounds into the belly of my Kamado Joe grill. With a match or a lighter (I don't even use fluid!) I can have those coals glowing in minutes, control the temperature with airflow, and turn out the food perfectly every time.

My grill cost a bit more than my father's did, but the Big Joe will never rust, nobody will ever steal it (365 pounds), and the meals—that actually taste like they were cooked outdoors—would make my daddy very proud.

Fifteen

A SALTY DETAIL

Just checking before we go much further . . . So far, we have scattered quite a few dots. You *are* keeping all of them, right? I hope so. Don't overlook any. They'll begin to connect for you soon.

As the dots link up, you'll gain an amazing ability to decode the information we've collected. Some of it, I'm sure, you've probably taken at face value. Soon, however, in many areas of your life, you'll possess the ability to quickly determine whether or not what everyone else has proclaimed to be *true* . . . is actually *the truth*. That, as you already know, is a bottom-of-the-pool kind of thing!

At first, the dots will more quickly connect in your Location of Contemplation. That special place will provide the quiet allowing you to fully engage the level of concentration needed at first. Before long, however, dot connecting will become second nature.

The difference in what is true and the truth will become rather obvious to you, seemingly without the difficult search your mind has had to embark upon in the past.

At that time you will begin applying the wisdom gained by making that distinction to virtually every part of your life. During conversations, you'll learn to naturally calculate the human equation revealed by the difference. In turn, the value you bring to relationships—even those of long standing—will soar.

The gap between what is true and the truth will become apparent in every business meeting you attend. This thought process will be available in both your quietest and craziest of times. Often, it will lead to life-changing levels of insight that progress into wisdom you will be able to explain and share with others.

When you task this true/truth paradox to be used as a filter, the answers you discover—even answers to questions no one has asked—will be plain to see. Once examined, confirmed, and harnessed, the difference in what others understand to be true versus what you know to be the truth . . . will have the power to dramatically change the results you have come to expect in your professional and personal life.

One critical point:

> **This application will produce extraordinary results that are available to *you* only because society is virtually blind to the enormous consequence of continuing to ignore one tiny detail about competition.**

This tiny detail is a basic life principle. It was discovered at the bottom of the pool and has become the secret key to competing in a way your competition doesn't even know a game is going on.

Surely, you must be thinking, *if it were this simple, wouldn't everyone already know?* Perhaps the best explanation of the thought process might be a consideration of salt.

Without a doubt, salt improves the taste of the things you eat. But if you'd never experienced salt—if you did not know salt existed—would you miss it? Would you note its absence? No, of course not. Yet you would still enjoy *food*.

If you and I had not determined to think to the bottom of the pool . . . if we'd never begun to examine the difference between what is *true* and *the truth*—if we had never said a word—I am convinced that no one would have ever missed it.

But in not having missed it, they would have missed EVERYTHING.

Everything? Define *everything*.

In this case *everything* refers to "unrecognized potential." And somewhere at the far end of that unrecognized potential lies a point that really is the peak of production. That rather small, sparsely populated area is, in reality, the highest level of accomplishment. We call that place THE BEST.

Is it possible to be satisfied you have done *your* best and never even come close to accomplishing THE BEST?

Of course. Phrases such as "at peace with the situation" or "satisfied with my performance" are simply the adult way of describing the feeling we kids had long ago at the surface of the

If you and I had not determined to think to the bottom of the pool . . . if we'd never begun to examine the difference between what is *true* and *the truth*—if we had never said a word—I am convinced that no one would have ever missed it.

But in not having missed it, they would have missed EVERYTHING.

pool. Remember? Because we knew we were doing the best we could do—and since we were not aware of any possible higher level of accomplishment—we never searched beyond what we were doing!

What's the point about salt?

It's just an easily understood analogy. If you prefer, we could use tomatoes . . .

Go with salt? Okay . . . for a moment, imagine a world without salt. Salt has never been tasted or used in any way. In that world, are people discontent? No. Why? Because they live in a world without salt.

Do they feel something is missing? Have they begun to believe they've been deprived? No, of course not. They live in a world without salt.

The people have lived for generations without even knowing salt existed. In fact, for them, salt doesn't exist. Therefore, their world—the way their food tastes, how they preserve meat and fish, their methods for removing ice—is perfectly acceptable. A lack of salt creates no angst among the world's population, for not only has no one ever seen it or tasted it . . . no one has ever imagined it!

Now, suppose salt is introduced into that world. After a short period of time, do people prefer their food with salt? Yes.

Do they discover salt preserves fish more efficiently and keeps fish edible longer than their previous method of preserving fish . . . which was to put it outside in the sun? Yes.

As opposed to cracking ice with a pickax and removing it with a shovel and wheelbarrow, do they now prefer salt as an easier tool for removing ice from a driveway? Yes. Yes, they do.

So while it is true that a world without salt is acceptable, the truth is that a world *with* salt is extraordinary.

But you still want to know about the tomato? Sure . . .

The tomato plant is a member of the deadly nightshade family and was considered poisonous for more than two hundred years. Northern Europeans and American colonists held fast to the belief that the tomato plant was highly toxic. And it was. Who could argue the fact? No one. For many people had seen dogs and cattle die after eating the tomato.

That the tomato plant is toxic remains an undisputed fact to this day. It is absolutely true that the tomato plant is poisonous. *True* . . . but not *the truth*.

As it turns out, only the stalk and green leaves of the plant are dangerous. And even then, only if a large quantity of them is consumed. The fruit of the tomato plant, as you already know, is not only edible but delicious.

It was Robert Gibbon Johnson who almost single-handedly turned the tide of poisonous public perception in 1820, when he mounted a stage in front of the Old Salem County Courthouse and, with a gathered audience of onlookers, calmly ate a small basket of tomatoes. The crowd waited for Johnson to die. He did not.

That the tomato plant is poisonous is true. It's just not the truth. More often than not, people cease any search when arriving at what is true. Why? Because it's true! They believe what they have found to be *the* answer. The proof they offer to themselves as confirmation is that the answer they have found produces results.

Remember what we discussed in chapter 6? The higher the achiever—the closer to the top of any field of endeavor one is acknowledged to be—*because of the results they have already produced*, the less likely they are to attempt thinking beyond what got them there in the first place.

You and I, however, do not stop at the discovery of true. It may be *an* answer but it is not *the* answer. True can and often does produce great results. But they are not THE BEST results.

True, once found, locates itself on the surface of the pool where it can be spotted easily, even by the crowds casually looking for an answer. The truth—THE BEST—is oftentimes easily seen but only by those who are looking and only those who are looking in the right place.

The right place to look . . . is a location beyond where everyone else has stopped. When everyone seems to be living it up on the surface, the truth is waiting for you at the bottom of the pool.

Sixteen

DISCOVERING THE TRUTH ABOUT MYSELF

I've told you the story of the bottom of the pool and how it began to make sense. But have you wondered how I came to understand the dollars-and-cents side of the equation?

Well, the answer has to do with having learned that before jumping out there with big advice for you, I'd better experiment on myself first. From the bottom of the pool, I began to uncover the beginnings of something that appeared to be unrecognized by modern society. You and I have already discussed it—the fact that something can be true yet still not be the truth.

The truth, I believed, and as you know, indicated the presence of a foundation, a pure and unfiltered reality that cannot from that particular point be redirected or explained further.

Earlier I described part of the thought process I utilize in determining whether or not I might be able to help a corporation, business, or team. I stated that the final measure I must make about the people in key leadership positions is to ask, "Will they go with me to the bottom of the pool?"

The answer to this question is quite obviously a determination I must make about a potential client. But the reason I must answer this question accurately has to do with someone else entirely. Me.

That's right. The someone else is me. At first glance (just a heads-up here), the thinking I am about to detail might appear to be contradictory, but slow down, stay with me. We are about to examine another mostly undiscovered or totally ignored detail that, once understood, will make a massive difference in your professional life.

The degree to which you will ever be financially compensated is inexorably linked to the obvious greater value (OGV) that you create for someone else.

In seeking to discern whether or not a potential client will be willing to go with me to the bottom of the pool, it is crucial that determination be made with the most unencumbered thinking I can muster. I must guard against being swayed by any feelings of affection for the potential client or financial offers they might make.

Their willingness to go to the bottom of the pool must be the final arbiter in my decision. If for any other reason, I have found, as the old saying goes, then I'm just asking for trouble.

When any part of the leadership of an organization is satisfied to compete on the surface—no matter what they might otherwise proclaim publicly—I have never seen the organization achieve more than an average, industry-standard increase in results. Unfortunately, this is the case even when a leader is publicly promising his peers one thing while privately thinking and doing another.

An example of this (a real one) is an advance meeting I once had with a potential client. It was early in my career of accepting this type of yearly challenge. And to that point, everyone with whom I had worked produced incredible results. The meeting that day included the CEO and her three senior-level vice presidents. As we began, I quickly explained how, if we came to an agreement, we would immediately begin to compete at a level on which their competition would not even know a game was being played.

As the meeting progressed, I explained why it was necessary to me that the specific goal we accomplished within a calendar year was that the organization double its results. At least. I made sure (I thought) that they understood how important this result was to me. And as I will explain to you later in this chapter, I carefully informed them why doubling their previous year's revenue was important to me. It was not because of who I was. No, it was important because of who I was *not*.

All four leaders were outwardly enthusiastic and agreed that doubling the numbers of the previous year was necessary. They understood why it had to be done, and the fact that I had shown them how it *would* be done, they claimed, gave them total confidence. They were ready to go.

It wasn't until much later that I discovered one of the vice presidents, despite the enthusiastic appearance to his boss (and to me), was not really on board after all. In fact, almost immediately after we hit the go button, he started a narrative that quietly destroyed the effort. It went like this:

> "Well, you are aware, of course, that nobody has ever actually doubled, right? Still, it's a good exercise for everyone. It will give us all experience setting appropriate goals . . .
>
> "You know, when you think about it (Ha! Ha! Ha!), if we really *did* double, it would be a disaster. I mean, how would we handle the business? Can you imagine how insane the workload would become?"

The other three leaders didn't understand what was happening until it was too late. I learned my lesson too. On the top deck, it is easy to believe what one sees is the same throughout the ship. But if one of the officers has slipped below and drilled a hole in the hull, smooth sailing is only an illusion.

Today, well before broaching the possibility of a client relationship with any leader or group of leaders, I watch carefully for character traits—both good and bad. I watch for enthusiasm, humility, openness, arrogance, curiosity, an eagerness to learn, an engaged sense of humor, a determination to understand, a willingness to listen, joyfulness, flexibility, self-control, fear, a wise perspective, imagination, a servant's spirit, and (here is a big one to me) the ability to focus on what an ordinary person is saying even while the governor of the state waits to say hello.

In any case, as I stated, I must be completely honest with myself about who they really are. I also now understand that the most critical reason I must be accurate in my assessment of them . . . is me.

As strange as it may seem, this part of the decision has very little to do with who I think I am. Instead—as I also stated earlier—it has a whole lot to do with who I've realized I am not!

I am not an Olympic gold medalist. I do not have a Super Bowl ring. I was never the hero of some national disaster who ended up on the cover of *Time*. I've not been the CEO of a famous corporation. I am not a television actor or a movie star.

I am, however, probably a lot like you. You pay close attention to increasing your family's financial security. Yeah, me too.

For years I was aware that the kinds of people I listed above were sometimes paid twenty or thirty times what anyone ever considered offering me for a comparable hour of time. The financial gap between us never really bothered me. After all, they had done things that made them famous. I was not famous. So, no worries. It was what it was.

And what it *was* . . . was true.

Retired quarterbacks and former gymnasts were worth a lot more than Andy Andrews. Experts in the speaking industry had long before determined that I had maxed out at the highest level someone like me would ever be paid. (And trust me, it wasn't a whole lot.)

Yes, it *was* true. Fortunately I managed to figure out that it wasn't the truth. I didn't know it then, but I was competing on the surface of the pool . . . treading water for all I was worth. Today I don't know whether to be embarrassed or not, but I swam around blindly for years before understanding something so simple that the fact I missed it still seems ridiculous.

The breakthrough was not sudden. Nothing came to me like a light being switched on. Rather, it was a struggle to the bottom of *that* pool. Slowly I began to understand that to be paid like a Hall of Fame quarterback, it wasn't necessary that I have Super Bowl rings. The only thing I had to do was become as valuable to an organization as the quarterback had been to his team!

To a corporation, I asked myself, what *is* the value of a Hall of Fame quarterback? The answers I came up with boiled down to celebrity factor (everyone could have their picture made with him) and inspiring stories from his NFL career. And the quarterback would relate those stories to character, preparedness, persistence, and all the things every other speaker (including me) talked about every time they hit the stage.

I knew I couldn't compete with the quarterback's celebrity, and as far as speaking skill or even content, it didn't matter. As far as I could see—minus the personal stories used to illustrate things like "having a good attitude"—most corporate speakers already delivered material that was very similar. That included the quarterback and me.

Knowing his celebrity trumped my content and believing myself unlikely to vault into celebrityhood (is that a word?), I realized there was only one avenue available to someone like me.

I had to create content that would trump celebrity. That meant I would need to seek wisdom and understanding like I had never before done in my life. Not only would I need to compete with the value of celebrity; I determined I would need to create content that could overpower the financial fear corporations display during a national economic downturn.

How, you ask, might that even be possible? I decided it all boiled down to the value of the content. And because I was the one who had to come up with something beyond what every speaker in the world was saying, in reality, it was the value of *me* that was on the line.

I'm ashamed to say that before that time, I never went after the truth about myself. You see, I had always thought of my career in terms of what I *would* be paid or what I thought I *should* be paid.

It never occurred to me to be honest with myself about what I was actually worth.

I realized (with a blinding flash of the obvious) that I had to become more valuable. Moreover, because I did not possess Super Bowl rings or gold medals, the value I brought to the game would need to be obvious and the results would have to be provable.

With specific teaching and unorthodox but logical strategies, if I could become someone capable of helping a company or team achieve dramatic results—*real quantifiable results* that none of them had ever dared imagine—only then would my own world change.

Sixteen and a half

NOT EVEN A FULL TURN

Some years ago there was a mechanic who was (at least once) paid ten thousand dollars for less than a minute's physical labor. It happened on the fabrication floor of a major manufacturer where the production of several hundred employees relied upon one massive machine that geared and ran the company's assembly line.

One morning the owner of the company was awakened to the news that this critical device had broken down. Hundreds of workers were idle. The owner rushed to the plant in a panic. The men and women at this factory typically produced almost a million dollars in product every day, but on this day, everything was at a standstill.

The owner made it to the assembly floor and was being briefed by shift foremen just before help arrived. Today we would call him a technician, but at that time our hero was referred to as "merely" a mechanic.

The idled workforce gathered as the mechanic walked around the big machine. They were quiet, straining to hear the soft questions the man asked their foreman. In what seemed like no time at all, the mechanic retrieved a pair of long-handled pliers from his bag.

Approaching the machine, dragging a tall stool, he paused only for a moment. At the base of the massive apparatus, the mechanic climbed atop the stool. Not once did he take his eyes from something he had spotted amidst the jumble of bolts, levers, tubes, valves, wires, and circuits. Standing straight, he reached above his head with the pliers. Easing them around a breaker board and between a tangle of yellow connectors, he firmly gripped the head of a small hex screw.

Closing his eyes, the mechanic carefully turned the screw one half revolution. He paused, waited, and then turned it just a tiny bit more. Opening his eyes as he pulled the pliers away, he looked at the screw and rubbed it once with his finger.

"Start her up," he said to one of the foremen. And they did. As the machine roared to life, a big cheer went up, the assembly line started moving, and the workers literally ran to their stations.

Moments later the owner and several executives were discussing the morning's event when the mechanic approached. "How much do I owe you?" the owner said as he pulled his checkbook from his jacket pocket.

The mechanic smiled. "That will be ten thousand dollars, sir."

Almost having a stroke, the owner sputtered, "That's absolutely ridiculous! Why, you only worked for a minute. I won't even consider it without a written bill, itemized, detailing the charge and justifying the amount." Pointing a finger, he added, "All you did was turn a single screw!" And with that, he moved to go.

"Sir," the mechanic called over the noise of the machine. "Sir, if you will . . ." The owner stopped, half turning to see if the man had come to his senses. "Sir," the mechanic said, "I can have the bill for you very quickly."

Already he had removed a pen and statement book from his bag. Scribbling briefly, the mechanic carefully tore the page from his book and presented the bill to the owner. "My business information is at the bottom, sir. Please send the check to me at that address."

As the mechanic walked away, the owner unfolded the bill. With his executives angling for a look as well, the owner read:

Turning one screw		$5.00
Knowing which screw to turn,		
knowing the direction to turn it,		
and knowing how far to turn it		$9,995.00
Total		$10,000.00
The service call is complimentary. Thank you, sir, for allowing me to help.		

By the time the owner had gotten back to his office, he agreed with the bill. The mechanic was paid promptly.

What is the moral of the story? Simply this:

The degree to which you will ever be financially compensated is inexorably linked to the obvious greater value (OGV) that you create for someone else.

STOP!

—Please Be Aware—

The intense analysis in the following chapter is a careful dissection of words intended to transform the alarm bells of financial opportunity (currently being ignored by a generation) into a good old-fashioned heads-up from me to you.

Seventeen

THE OGV AND YOUR FUTURE

The degree to which you will ever be financially compensated is inexorably linked to the obvious greater value (OGV) that you create for someone else.

I want to tell you how this sentence affected my life, and I will, but at this point I fear you might view the story as mere conversation. What I really desire to convey is how this sentence can affect *your* life.

Therefore, it's important that we break this sentence down. Read slowly. Read carefully. Let's use our own bottom-of-the-pool version of reverse engineering, start from the beginning, and rebuild the sentence a little bit at a time.

THE WORDS: *The degree*

THE MEANING: *How much*

THE WORDS: *The degree to which you will be financially compensated*

THE MEANING: *How much money you will make*

Wait. Yeah, we need to back up. It'll only take a minute, but I left out the word *ever.* Let's try that one again.

THE WORDS*: The degree to which you will* ever *be financially compensated*

THE MEANING*: Always. Without exception.*

Sorry we had to go back, but I *did* miss the "ever." It's a common mistake. Most people do. But I know better, so there's no excuse for my blunder. Again, I'm sorry . . . but, simply put . . .

One cannot ever miss the "ever."

The word *ever* in the sentence changes the entire meaning, not to mention adding a critical level of importance to the concept. That single word acts as its own triple exclamation point, blaring a wake-up call to EVERyone who wants to achieve more. It pertains to EVERything. It concerns forEVER. As in: for the rest of your life.

THE WORDS: *The degree to which you will ever be financially compensated is inexorably linked*

THE MEANING: *The amount of money you make for the rest of your life is not dependent upon a roll of the dice.*

There is something you can do to determine your degree of financial independence. There is something you can do to determine your level of prosperity. Furthermore, you actually possess the ability to control how quickly the money comes in, how much of it there is, and how long that income stream continues.

However . . . your ability to control these things is inexorably linked to (or "depends absolutely and unequivocally upon") something else. Fortunately that "something else" is already within your control.

Most people live their whole lives experiencing the combined feelings of stress and helplessness. Unfortunately, they never know any of the things you and I are thinking through right now. Even though it has the power to effectively eliminate their feelings of stress and helplessness. Why? Because thoroughly learning anything with the power to change how we live and coming to understand exactly how to harness that power are tough.

A functional understanding of any principle capable of yielding peace, influence, and prosperity simply requires deeper concentration for longer periods of time than most people are willing to invest. The potential return on investment is not considered. In fact, for many people nothing is considered. Because the sad truth is:

They just don't want to think this hard.

For you, however, regarding any confusion or desire for escape you might be experiencing at the moment—be calm. Understand that the pressure in your head is normal. This is just what it feels like when you go deeper. So, don't stop here. And for God's sake, don't look up or pause for a breath. Bear down. Focus.

We are closing in on the bottom of the pool.

THE WORDS: *The degree to which you will ever be financially compensated is inexorably linked to the greater value you create for someone else.*

THE MEANING: *According to the dictionary, the word* valuable *means "extremely useful or important; worth a great deal of money." Therefore, in order to create value for other people, you must do, provide, or become something that is extremely useful or important. Because that is worth money. Creating* greater *value is worth more money . . . correct? It certainly should be.*

Keep reading.

Knowing that you have the power to choose every moment of every day, what you do with your time is entirely up to you. You can invest it wisely or waste it foolishly. By choosing how to invest your time, it follows that you are also choosing what you learn, how much you learn, how deeply you understand what you've learned, what your imagination makes of it, and in what fashion you act upon whatever that might be.

Fundamentally this is the choice that determines who you become. Because *how you think* determines *who you are*, it also determines *who you are becoming* and *who you ultimately become*.

In other words, there is no need to live your life as a pawn of circumstance, for *who* you become has authority over *what* you become. And what you become—whether a wise and prosperous leader, generous to your fellow man, or a complaining bum—will be an accurate indication of the value you are creating.

Wait. . . . Well, I did it again. So sorry, but once more I have failed to include a key word in the quote. And the do-over is:

THE WORDS: *The degree to which you will ever be financially compensated is inexorably linked to the* obvious *greater value you create for someone else.*

THE MEANING: *Plain to see. Unable to be missed. Conspicuous. Incontestable.*

Beyond doubt. As clear as day.

Admittedly, while overlooking the word *obvious* is a bit ironic, the real difference its omission makes is no laughing matter.

Suppose there are two business owners providing the same service in the same area of town. On the surface they appear to offer the same service at the same price. But they don't. In fact, while one business owner provides value for his customers, the other provides greater value. Which owner gets your business? Not so fast . . . it's a trick question.

Every day, all over the world, people are deciding who to hire, where to shop, what church to attend, which dentist, what Realtor . . .

They make hundreds of choices from the endless categories derived from four basic areas of life—goods, services, people, and places. This teenager or that one? This restaurant or the one down the street? The new place at the mall or the old place downtown?

It's all rhetoric, of course, until the choice all those people are making is between someone else . . . or you.

> Because *how you think* determines *who you are*, it also determines *who you are becoming* and *who you ultimately become.*

On the surface choices of this kind would appear to be simple and straightforward. The millions of people answering these questions every day provide astonishing evidence that we don't always choose the greater value in all situations. Or even in most situations. The truth? It's a coin flip.

"What!" you are probably saying in disbelief. "You must be

joking. How is that possible? You are saying that a lot of us don't automatically choose the greater value?"

Yes, I am saying that. Left to our own devices, most of us choose the greater value only about 50 percent of the time.

Why?

For the simple reason that most of us never recognize the greater value. We don't discern the difference. And that is why *the greater value must be obvious.*

We don't consider the fact often, but in reality most of us are experts in only a couple or three of life's categories. In our areas of expertise it is usually easy to determine the difference in value and greater value. Usually.

Outside those specific areas, however, because we possess only a casual knowledge about almost everything else, greater value is tougher to spot. Therefore, if you are competing in any way, shape, or form that requires a human being to make a choice, be aware that while actually providing greater value is necessary and commendable, it's *not nearly enough* to win.

Bottom of the pool: if you want folks to choose you—each and every time—then the greater value you have created had better be obvious.

Eighteen

COMPETING IN DEEP WATER

Most likely you've already made the connection I am about to mention. Before continuing, however, I want to be certain. While the examples used as we explore this topic are about business, the application is much broader. In reality, the essence of competition in life *is* the message.

Your personal life and your professional life have so much effect on each other, you might as well consider them as one.

Unfortunately (for them) most people live their entire lives without the slightest awareness that they are competing every day. Worse, for many of them, a total description of how they are *already* competing would do no good, for they wouldn't believe it in the first place or would zone out before hearing the entire explanation.

Again, they just don't want to think that hard.

In a weird way, I suppose, as bad as it is for them, it is certainly good news for you. It's as if your opponent arrived at the stadium but spent the whole contest sitting in the stands. Seriously, if that were literally the case . . . how easy would it be to win *that* game?

Do you remember when I told you that I teach clients to compete at a level on which the competition doesn't even know a game is being played? Before we get into what "obvious value" actually is, allow me to address a misconception in the marketplace. If you are already a business owner, brace yourself. What I am about to reveal might be a shock to your system. Here goes . . .

For a moment set aside the concept of obvious value.

Even the dullest business mind is at least vaguely aware that the perception of value creates a feeling of satisfaction. When a business creates value for its clients or customers, its goal—most often—is that the client or customer be satisfied.

Unfortunately the goal of having satisfied customers is the worst kind of trap, one that is particularly devastating because most businesses set it, bait it, and charge into it willingly. And because they enjoy the camaraderie (after all, everyone else is trying to get in there too), they stay in the trap forever.

You might be interested to know that when I agree to align myself with a company or organization, the very first thing I make clear is that *the business of customer satisfaction is no way to attract new customers or keep your old ones.*

Most companies, without some outside source sending a

shock wave through their system, never even glance *beyond* what to them seems like the ultimate goal—satisfying each and every customer.

Okay, okay, okay . . . I can hear your head exploding from here. Settle down and let's think through this. Is it necessary that a business satisfy its customers? Yes. Yes, it is necessary. That is true. But you and I are exploring the bottom of the pool, where the truth reveals much more.

QUESTION: For satisfying every customer during the month of June, what reward does a business receive?

TRUE ANSWER: All salaries are paid, occasionally with bonuses. In addition, there is acknowledgment in the community that this business is one of the area's best.

Okay . . . Let's try this again . . .

QUESTION: For satisfying every customer during the month of June, what reward does a business receive?

THE TRUTH: They get to do it again in July!

Know this:

"Customer satisfaction" is the lowest bar you can possibly hit and still stay in business.

Anything less and you are in trouble.

QUESTION: How does the typical consumer view the concept of customer satisfaction?

TRUE ANSWER: "I don't really think about it a lot. I suppose I have a bit more appreciation for the businesses that pay attention to that kind of thing."

Again . . . with a tinge more to the question as well.

QUESTION: Deep in his or her subconscious, how does the typical consumer *really* view the concept of customer satisfaction as it relates to them?

THE TRUTH: "I had better be satisfied. I paid for it."

Know this:

Assuming this answer reflects a common feeling, a business focused on customer satisfaction as the ultimate goal is competing for its life in a way its leaders believe is an advantage over competitors.

Unfortunately, through the years, though numbers and percentages of numbers have been carefully recorded, extensively calculated, and analyzed, that advantage has proven to be a lot like vapor. It sure looks like something, but when you grab it, there's nothing there.

If you are a business owner competing with your rivals and you believe customer satisfaction is your secret advantage over them, you are mistaken. Because they are competing against you in the same manner.

THINK: Your product is the same. Your prices are virtually the same. If customer satisfaction is what you are depending upon to be the difference maker—if that's how you have decided to separate your business from the pack—in reality you have only one chance of that happening. As you work to satisfy your customers, you can only hope your competitors fail to satisfy theirs.

"Customer satisfaction" is the lowest bar you can possibly hit and still stay in business.

To have a shot at results that seem impossible to most, you must learn to compete in a way that your competitors do not even know there is a game going on.

YOUR QUESTION: "Come on, Andy. No exaggerations, please. I need you to be serious. How likely is it—in reality—that I might actually be able to compete with some kind of an advantage that my business rivals don't know about?"

MY ANSWER: *Very* likely. In fact, it's as close to a sure thing as I have ever come to understand. One caveat, however . . . I never said you'd have an advantage your business rivals didn't know about. I said you could compete on a level that they wouldn't know a game was being played. You see, your competitors will be well aware of the advantage you'll soon employ. But as unbelievable as it may seem, they will most likely be completely blind to its overwhelming power.

Before revealing exactly what that power is, I'd like *you* to answer three extremely important questions.

1. Have you ever paid more for something than you had to?
   TO BE CLEAR: Even though you were aware the product or service could have been purchased at a lower price somewhere else, you elected to buy it at a higher price.
2. Have you ever made a purchase and, in doing so, driven farther or gone to more trouble than was absolutely necessary?
   TO BE CLEAR: You could have bought it down the street, but you chose to drive across town in order to purchase the same thing.
3. Have you ever paid more for something while going to more trouble to get it?
   TO BE CLEAR: You could have purchased the item online and paid less, but you chose to drive to a brick-and-mortar store and pay more.

Let me guess.

Yes, yes, and yes. Right? Of course. And you aren't remotely alone. It would be a safe bet that almost all of us answered the questions just as you did.

But wait. Don't we consider ourselves fairly intelligent? I mean, we don't brag about it, but we have managed to navigate our lives on a reasonably steady course. Paying more for something than we have to, however, doesn't seem very smart.

In fact, now that I think about it, it's ridiculous. I'm embarrassed. You? After thinking through the two choices available, how stupid does someone have to be in order to come to this decision: "Yes, I know I can buy it for less money. I am aware that I can do so with very little time or effort on my part. But *no*! I want to pay more for it and go to more trouble getting it!"

Does this make sense to you? How in the world is it possible that millions of us could independently arrive at a decision like that—to behave in a manner that not only disregards common sense but defies logic? And get this: we happily admit it and will probably do it again before next week!

No, it doesn't make sense. Or maybe I should say that it doesn't make sense . . . on the surface. On the surface, you see, everyone competes in almost exactly the same way.

On the surface, games are contested over price and product.

Have you noticed how often McDonald's and Burger King locations are within a stone's throw of each other? Oh yeah, they aren't just watching each other on the New York Stock Exchange. They are keeping their eyes focused on price and product—their own and that of the competition.

The same goes with Walgreens and CVS. Family Dollar and Dollar General. Starbucks and Dunkin' Donuts. Even gas stations and automobile dealerships locate as close as they can get to their competitors.

The next time you see the manager of your local Shell station climb a ladder to change the gas price on his sign, pull out your stopwatch and punch the stem. You don't think the Exxon lady next door and the BP guy across the street are watching? Most likely, their signs will be changed within the hour. The essence of their battle for market share is price and product.

Home Depot and Lowe's build their stores close to each other more often than not. In addition, each store regularly sends teams into the other. Their mission? To bring back information on specific brands being carried and how much the items cost. That's right . . . price and product.

On the surface, games are contested over price and product.

But that's on the surface. A business (or a team, a church, a city, a family, a state, and so on) competing from the bottom of the pool, however, can acquire a virtually unbeatable edge.

Even though potential customers most often see competitors (and their products and services) as essentially the same, there remains a seldom-seen, supremely compelling inside track the potential customer will always take if given half a chance.

It is a foundational game-changer that easily trumps the allure of a lower price. This rarely experienced but completely overpowering advantage is called the *obvious greater value* (OGV).

You see, the products being carried and how much to charge for them are virtually the only things your competitors consider.

They may talk about customer service, but all that means to most of them is that their business had the product the customer was looking for in stock at a price that didn't make the customer go somewhere else. And as long as no employee was rude while the customer was in the store, as far as your competitors are concerned, that customer was "satisfied."

What your competitors never consider is the dot you and I are now connecting.

While aware of the importance of what they refer to as *their* customer service, your competitors remain blind to the overwhelming power wielded by what they refer to as *your* customer service. The obvious greater value provided by you and those on your team become a distinct and unequaled brand when every part of your business is delivered in a package of genuine care, personal concern, and honest connection.

Nineteen

THE INVISIBLE, UNCONTESTABLE EDGE

If you have read this far, whether or not you have even acknowledged it to yourself, you have a hunger to win. Some of us are interested in winning football games. Some of us want to win souls. Some deeply desire to win as a parent. Others want to win in business or in a combination of several things.

It seems almost beyond the realm of possibility to conceive of a single answer with the power to gain wins in virtually every category of life being contested, but the answer is real, and it is available to you.

There are those in life who consistently avoid problems. Unaware of the hidden repercussions, they also avoid many long-term benefits the answers to those problems might have provided had they faced the problems in the first place. And of course, avoiding problems is like ignoring weeds. They get bigger and they multiply.

There are also many people who only do what they have to do. They deal with as much as they must in order to remain afloat. For these folks, as long as the answers they find allow them to tread water, that is enough. They never find great answers because it's too much work; it takes too much time, and frankly, *again*, they just don't want to think that hard.

Oddly enough, it's usually not the answer that requires deep thought; it's the question. Great questions that you ask yourself will send your conscious mind *and* your subconscious mind on a search for wisdom and perspective that can ultimately yield life-changing answers.

Never forget:

The quality of your answers will usually be determined by the quality of your questions.

Fortunately for us, we asked a truly great question in the previous chapter. Remember? We established that despite knowing a product or service is easily available at a lower cost, the vast majority of us have and will continue to occasionally jump through more hoops and pay a higher price in certain situations.

Here's the question we asked: How in the world is it possible that millions of us would independently arrive at a decision like that—to behave in a manner that not only disregards common sense but defies logic? The answer comes straight from the bottom of the pool.

There is a single common denominator uniting the decisions each of us made separately to spend our money in what, at first glance, appears to be such an illogical manner. Deepening the mysterious nature of our actions is the fact that the common denominator is, by itself, completely logical. In other words, while none of us talked to each other about what we had done, we all had a good reason for doing it.

The reason we willingly paid more and went to more trouble to do so is incredibly clear and makes perfect sense. At least, it makes perfect sense once you know the answer.

In each instance our actions were (and continue to be) a tangible way in which we demonstrate gratefulness or loyalty. And in every case, that someone, at some point, did something so special for us or became so important to us that we would never think of doing business anywhere else.

Who they are and what they have done is so powerful that it trumps price, distance, and time. That person overcame any tendency we might have had to allow price to determine our behavior. Whether inadvertently or on purpose, they created greater value in our lives. And it was obvious.

Never confuse greater value with *obvious* greater value. Though the distinction may seem subtle (or even nonexistent to some), the two are as different as night and day. Note that many of us have prescriptions filled at the closest chain store pharmacy. The decision to do so is most often driven by a casual perception of value. Even for greater value, however, most of us will not make a significant effort to shop elsewhere.

Nevertheless, we *will* drive all the way across town to the small independent pharmacy and happily pay more for the same product if the greater value is obvious.

Most often we perceive greater value in terms of price or convenience or both. Obvious greater value is usually proven. We are convinced of the OGV by a realization about what is truly important in our lives.

Consider that we occasionally change our minds about who cuts our hair. How well they cut it, how consistently, their availability, the price, the personality of the hair stylist, wait times—a lot can factor into how we unconsciously calculate the value of that haircut.

On the other hand, if a hair stylist provides obvious greater value, we might have that person cut our hair for the rest of our lives and never once consider anyone else. For obvious greater value, we would happily pay more. And the haircut does not even have to be that great.

Most often we perceive greater value in terms of price or convenience or both. Obvious greater value is usually proven. We are convinced of the OGV by a realization about what is truly important in our lives.

Here are two real-life examples of obvious greater value. The first concerns the small independent pharmacy; the second, a hair stylist. Both are presented in a way that you hear only one side of the conversation.

"Oh sure, I know it costs a little more to get our medicine at Vandavender's Drugstore. And no, it's not just around the corner. But I have to say that, for me, it's worth it. You know Roy, of course? The pharmacist? Listen. When I go in there with my son, Roy comes out from behind the counter to shake hands . . . with him. My boy is six years old. Do you hear what I'm saying?

"Look . . . five days a week, my wife or I drive him to school. The principal stands outside every morning to greet the kids—fist-bumping every single one of them as they arrive. At church, our son is high-fived by the pastor and every other man there. They all high-five him. The kid has been high-fived by almost every adult he's seen since he started walking!

"Then he played T-ball this year. His coach taught him a sign to flash—it's something he does with his hand. And now, all the parents of the other kids do the sign too. Ugh.

"My point is this: When my son grows up, no one is ever going to hire him because he can high-five. He will never receive a promotion or a raise because he can fist-bump. My son needs to learn how to shake hands like a man, and for that to happen, his dad cannot be the only person in town who ever shakes his hand!

"Roy Vandavender shakes his hand and says, 'Come on now . . . squeeze . . . there ya go, gimme that firm grip. That's it. Look me in the eye now . . . smile . . . what do we say? Nice to meet you . . . *good* to see you.'

"Anyway, I don't care if we have a prescription to be filled or not. Heck, we just buy something else. But two or three times a week, my wife or I will drive all the way over there just to get our son around Roy for less than five minutes."

Or how about this phone conversation?

"Yes, Frank. As a matter of fact, that *was* me coming out of Edna's, and before you ask, yes, I do get my hair cut there.

"Yes, I know it's a beauty shop. And no, I'm not the only guy in town getting his hair cut by Ms. Edna.

"What? No, I feel fine. Why?

"No, Frank. That's very funny, but I'm not sick.

"Yes, sometimes she *does* cut it too short, but every time that happens, it always grows out again. Strange how that works, isn't it?

"No, I'm not being a smart aleck. I'm just sayin' that the occasional subpar haircut is not that big of a deal.

"Just trying to be optimistic, Frank. What do you want to hear?

"Okay, it's more than occasional.

"Frank. I'm gonna hang up if you don't stop laughing.

"Yes, I know there are other people who cut hair, and no, I don't need any recommendations. Thanks.

"Why don't you ask me why I always have Ms. Edna cut my hair?

"Thank you. Okay, here's the reason: Fourteen years ago,

my mom was in a nursing home. Even with all the health issues she had, Mother was embarrassed for us to see her without her hair done.

"Dad could not have cared less, of course, but she wanted to look like she always had. After several months of regular visits, I went to see her one day, and she looked like she had gone to a beauty parlor. What had happened, though, was that the beauty parlor came to her.

"It took a little digging. I didn't even know Ms. Edna back then, but I found out she had been going to the nursing home after work, once a week, and doing my mother's hair. She did it every week for three years until Mama passed away. And would never take a dime.

"No . . . yes, I *tried* to pay her. And get this: she *still* goes to the nursing home. Two nights a week now; after working all day, she's there . . . cutting the men's hair and beautifying the ladies. She still won't let anyone pay. So I decided that she would have to take my money if I went to her shop for haircuts. Anyway, that's why she cuts my hair.

"For eleven years. And as far as I'm concerned, Ms. Edna will be cutting my hair until one of us dies. I'll never go anywhere else. I couldn't.

"Sure . . . I think that would be great.

"Yeah, just call her. I'm sure she can fit you in."

While on the subject of these examples, I'd like to make a critical connection. When Roy began shaking hands with a child, did he think of it as a way to create an advantage over his business rivals? That seems doubtful, doesn't it?

Neither do I believe Edna quietly cut hair at the nursing home in order to make more money. However, it is undeniable that both those things have happened. Roy had a business advantage. Edna made more money.

The lesson *available* to be learned is this: even when one produces a great result inadvertently, a bottom-of-the-pool understanding of *why* the result was produced will allow one to produce the same result on purpose.

When the result is produced on purpose, however, its flames are fanned by word of mouth, allowing them to take place over a wider area, in greater volume, and for an almost unlimited amount of time.

This is what I call "competing on a level at which your competition doesn't even know there is a game being played." The fuel needed to compete in this way depends first and foremost upon one's ability to understand and identify greater value for other people.

Then that greater value must be refined and enriched to the point that it is obvious. I have found this process to be almost exclusively a function of who a person has become. And who a person has become is either the obvious part of the greater value provided or the delivery vehicle for the rest of it.

The second paragraph of this chapter is a single sentence. Hopefully, the first half of that sentence conveys my understanding as to why a person might remain somewhat skeptical: "It seems almost beyond the realm of possibility to conceive of a single answer with the power to gain wins in virtually every category of life being contested."

With the second half of the sentence, knowing full well that the skepticism exists, you will no doubt notice that I take the opportunity to double down: "but the answer is real, and it is available to you."

At the bottom of the pool lies a stunning realization. Not only is the answer real. Not only is the answer available to you. The answer, in fact, IS you.

In a contest that, on the surface, appears to be evenly matched—by price or product, by rules, age, tradition, or talent level—*who you are* becomes the deciding factor to those making the decision. That decision is one that not only determines where people shop; it includes whether they will write a letter of reference, who gets to date their daughters, and a host of other things most people never consider. Like balls and strikes, fair or foul, holding or not.

More than a few times you and I have heard the announcer of a televised football game say, "The officials can call holding on any play they want." A close study of film shows the statement to be factual more often than not. For in that moving, close-together mass of humanity, who's to say someone is holding . . . or not? Therefore, in most cases, the officials throw the flag on only the most obvious cases of holding. Maybe.

When both teams are bound by the same rules, but knowing the officials can decide whether to call a penalty whenever they decide they have *seen* holding . . . would one team have an advantage over another if the officials liked that team more?

Is it possible that the officials of a football game might give the slightest edge to a group of guys (a team) who behave in a way they appreciate? If the officials react like any other human being, then, yes, it is possible.

Don't misunderstand. I am not for a minute intimating that an advantage of any kind is given on purpose. I am saying that actions of this kind are often the product of subconscious thought, and most of us lean *toward* people we like and *away from* those we don't.

So who are these officials anyway? By watching several games on television, one can easily determine who they are, at least on average. In college football the officials appear to be about fifty years of age. They are overwhelmingly clean-cut, seem to be professional people (white collar instead of blue collar), and are all men. They are of an age to have at least one teenager still living at home. Look closely . . . the vast majority are wearing wedding rings.

What does all this have to do with anything?

Think about it. What does that kind of person like? What does he dislike? We are talking about a fifty-year-old, clean-cut, professional man who is married and still raising a teenager. What type of behavior does this person approve? Disapprove?

The next time you notice the University of Alabama football team playing on television, watch at least the beginning of the game. The beginning of the game is when the players' individual photographs are shown onscreen. While many other teams are dressed in T-shirts or jerseys without pads, the Crimson Tide photographs show them in jackets and ties.

Most other teams scowl at the camera, striking intimidating poses. On the other hand, the Alabama players display wide, friendly smiles.

They are respectful to the officials and coaches—even coaches of the opposing team—before, during, and after a game. There are no celebratory demonstrations after a first down, no arguments on the sidelines about coaching decisions, no questioning the calls of officials.

It's not my place to say whether or not any of this actually makes a difference. However, what kind of player do you like? What kind of behavior do you want your teenager to emulate?

Nick Saban, the head coach of Alabama, is unquestionably the best in college football. That's not opinion but fact, based upon him having won more national championships than all other active coaches combined. If there is anyone in the sporting world who understands the benefits that accrue for everyone when a team displays good behavior, solid citizenship, and great character . . . it is Nick Saban. He competes in ways the competition doesn't even recognize a game being played.

Want a basketball example? How about the Jordan Effect? When Michael Jordan was in his prime with the Chicago Bulls, opposing coaches gave that name—the Jordan Effect—to what they were convinced had become an unfair phenomenon taking place game after game. And the national media advanced the notion. Their argument was that game officials were so in awe of Michael and his talent they wouldn't call fouls on him.

As the opposing coaches, their teams, their teams' fans, and the media became increasingly obsessed with the idea, someone actually monitored Chicago Bulls games for a while and "proved" that the Jordan Effect gave the Bulls at least a five-point advantage in every game they played. ESPN announcers often pointed out that referees were quick to call fouls on opposing players who were aggressive with Michael yet hesitant to call fouls on him when he was aggressive with opponents. On SportsCenter, viewers were shown video evidence of the many, many times Michael was allowed an extra step or two without dribbling and not called for traveling.

So it was true. The Jordan Effect was real.

However . . . the Jordan Effect actually had very little to do with Michael's mastery on the court. Michael Jordan had figured out how to compete in a way the competition didn't even understand a game was being played. Michael was already competing during warm-ups before the game. He was competing during TV time-outs. Occasionally he competed back at the hotel, before the team ever went to the arena. And his opponents had no clue.

If you've watched the NBA at all, you can't help but notice that many players react badly when called for a foul. Many times (most times?) they huff and puff and stare daggers at the official—antics that enrage their fans who often come up with abuse of their own to direct at the referee. During interviews after a game, it is commonplace to hear players criticize the officials.

But criticism and complaint were not in Jordan's repertoire.

Michael Jordan made sure he knew every referee by name and something about that official's life. And during the warm-ups, during TV time-outs, or in the lobby of the hotel, he'd talk.

"Steve!" he'd say. "How's your son? Bobby's in the eighth grade this year, right? I hear he's doing well on the court. Hey . . . you know I didn't even make the cut for my junior high team. Tell Bobby I said that he's doing better now than I did at his age! Tell him I said to keep after it!"

The official would get to go home and say, "By the way, Bobby . . . Michael said hello. Yes, of course we're friends. I'm sorry, I thought you knew that. Yeah, he calls me Steve."

There's your Jordan Effect. In game situations, who do you think received the benefit of the doubt? Was it the player griping about the calls, muttering curses under his breath every time he brushed by an official during the game? Or could it have been the ref's buddy—the guy who cared about his son?

This kind of competition can work both ways, of course.

John Hirschbeck was a Major League Baseball umpire for thirty-two years. John and his brother Mark were the first siblings ever to umpire in the major leagues.

It was nearing the end of the season on September 27, 1996. John Hirschbeck, already a hugely respected figure in baseball at the time, was the home plate umpire for a game between the Baltimore Orioles and Toronto Blue Jays. Sadly, he and his wife had recently suffered the loss of their eight-year-old son to a genetic brain disease (ALD). Then, in an almost unimaginable one-two punch, their second son was diagnosed with the same disorder.

That day, in his first at bat, Oriole second baseman Roberto Alomar struck out. The last pitch had been a called third strike. The player was enraged, arguing immediately and cursing the umpire. Then, to the stunned disbelief of everyone in the stadium and those at home watching on television, Alomar spit in John Hirschbeck's face.

I will spare you the details—including magazine covers and front-page newspaper accounts—that dogged the following weeks. Alomar was given an extremely light penalty that allowed him to play the next day and during his team's playoff appearances. The Major League Umpires Association, as you might imagine, were apoplectic that Alomar had not been immediately suspended from the league.

Amid all the hue and cry, however, there was a small group of people who watched the aftershocks of Alomar's disgusting gesture with fascination. Major league pitchers saw opportunity on the horizon. Why? Because they sensed—no, they *knew*—that the following season's strike zone for Alomar would expand to massive proportions. And it did.

As the 1997 season began, it became clear that all a pitcher needed to do was throw the ball *in the vicinity* of the plate. Often a pitch more than a foot off the plate, or one that Alomar needed to dodge in order to avoid being hit, would be called a strike by the umpire. And there was not a thing the Orioles, Major League Baseball, or Roberto Alomar could do about it. At the time there were no instant replay rules, and umpires, who were in total control, were allowed—as they would say—to "call 'em as I see 'em."

At the major league level, a ninety-five-mile-per-hour fastball moves from the pitcher's hand to the catcher's mitt in four-tenths of a second. Alomar, known at the time as one of the sharpest-eyed hitters in the game, was said to have been able to determine whether a pitch—even at that speed—was two inches *inside* the far edge of the plate or two inches *outside*. But because of a single display of incredibly bad manners in 1996, that phenomenal ability did not matter in 1997.

Able to patiently work the count for a walk ninety times in 1996, Alomar's total of "bases on balls" was reduced by more than half the following season. In 1997, he walked only forty times. In effect, those numbers show that while Roberto Alomar spit on only one umpire, he was subjected to a scrutiny the following year by *all* umpires who made it 56 percent tougher for him to get on base by way of a walk.

I suppose one could say the Alomar Effect was the exact opposite of the one for which Michael Jordan became known.

Before moving on, it is important to understand that these examples of sports at the highest levels, while true, are also effective metaphors for local youth league teams. In fact, on a local level, the individual or team that creates goodwill, exhibits great manners, and maintains a great reputation can experience greater game and life benefits than accrue to older, more accomplished players.

In that same light, knowing that the pharmacy and beauty shop we discussed are both small businesses, you should also be aware that the size of the business has no bearing on this competitive edge we've discovered at the bottom of the pool. A corporation with ten thousand employees is just as able to create incredible results as a small business with very few employees.

By understanding how to individually create OGV and connect who they are to their community and customers, a group of ten thousand can be as effective as a group of ten. I know that for sure because I worked with a company for three years that "got it" . . . they understood the power of obvious greater value from the beginning.

During those three years, I watched as the corporation grew from six hundred employees to ten thousand. In three years, they increased their annual revenue from $5.4 billion to beyond $22 billion.

They had and still have incredible leadership. The employees work hard in their individual efforts to build a better, stronger team every day. They encourage their team members and serve their fellow man openly in ways that have no connection to their actual business. The leaders are humble, fun, quick to handle situations before they become problems, and have made more friends outside their industry than most corporate leaders manage to do inside their own.

They *take* responsibility and *give* credit. Leadership like that is rare. It doesn't have to be, but it is.

Earlier we looked at a definition for the word *value*, and to help illustrate it is this sentence: "The antique chair has become quite valuable." The sentence is useful, I suppose, and does provide an answer for any fifth grader needing a definition on a vocabulary test. But for someone poking around as deeply as you and I are doing, there is more. And as usual, the simple question *Why?* will reveal the insight.

The antique chair has become more valuable over time? Okay . . . why? For the simple reason that as time passes, there are fewer and fewer chairs like that one. In effect, it has become rare. Scarcity is the first step on the road to rarity. The less of something there is, the rarer it becomes. And the rarer it becomes, the more valuable it is.

People like Roy and Edna and Nick and Michael—and you—are rare.

Twenty

MONEY IN GARBAGE

The obvious greater value (OGV) isn't used only in traditional business competition. OGV is a *business creator*, and young people everywhere are figuring this out.

In most cities, if a household wants its garbage picked up and hauled away, that garbage must be in large containers, waiting curbside, early in the morning, twice every week.

Eight times a month those big, heavy cans have to be hauled all the way to the street and, when they are emptied, hauled from the street back to the house. This chore must be performed in the stifling heat and humidity of summer in the Deep South.

It must be done in the Midwestern winter, struggling up or down steep driveways against the bitter wind or patches of ice. Despite the fact that it also occasionally rains, most residents in most cities do all this themselves. Or their children do it.

Some of those without children in their home eventually figure it is worth a few bucks to get the neighbor's kid involved in this process. Of course, we all know that this process with the neighbor's kid often involves a certain level of continued involvement.

Just like where you live, I'll bet, there aren't many situations a person can create in which they are able to put dealing with the garbage totally out of their minds. To find a neighbor's kid who never goes out of town, who doesn't occasionally have to be reminded or retaught, who doesn't have ball games or homework or a parent's emergency—well, that would be a rare kid.

Rare. As in valuable.

As it turns out, I know a kid who noticed that very thing. By examining the process of garbage removal and dealing with every single thing a homeowner has to remember or do, this young man has created value for a modest number of people. For now, he'd like to keep his name a secret, but he is readying for the time that his modest number of clients becomes a major number.

"When I go to work," he told me, "I do not look like a garbage man! I shower before I leave the house and dress like my clients are dressed when they leave for the office."

I've watched the young man work. He smiles and waves to the neighbors of his clients, and he smiles when he talks. This young man has created a high level of comfort and trust in the neighborhoods where he works. Value. And that value has also created a lot of curiosity.

"Who's the young man I see with your garbage cans?" a neighbor asked one of his clients. "Is he a student around here?

And where is he on his way to every time I see him? He sure isn't dressed for your garbage."

The client answered, "No, I don't suppose he is dressed for my garbage. But that's what he does. For a living, I mean. He created a business out of nothing. I pay him fifty-five dollars per month, and I never think about getting the garbage out anymore. I've never had to remind him. I've never had to ask that he do anything differently or pay closer attention. I do not think about it. I'm less stressed. I have more time on those mornings. My clothes are never messed up. Oh, you asked where he is on his way to? To the top, that's where. I'm going to get this guy as many customers as I can. I hope he makes a million dollars 'cause I don't *ever* want this young man to go away!"

He smiles and waves to the neighbors of his clients, and he smiles when he talks. This young man has created a high level of comfort and trust in the neighborhoods where he works. Value.

Now . . . that? That is several steps above mere greater value. That, my friend, is OBVIOUS GREATER VALUE.

It is interesting to me that when I tell the story of this young man, audiences seem to believe he was very smart to have hit upon this novel idea in the first place. In fact, what he is doing isn't a novel idea. My young friend was, however, smart enough to see something that had been done before, recognize that the business had started with one person, and figure out what fueled the success of that enterprise.

Remember the point in chapter 19 about ten thousand individuals able to be as effective as ten?

This young man is building the same type of business that Wayne Huizenga built and doing it in the same way. When Huizenga started Waste Management in 1968, it was a one-man operation. As he added employees, "the garbage man" placed a premium on treating customers like family. Today, Waste Management is valued at almost three billion dollars.

Twenty-one

A SMART MAN . . . AND A WISE ONE

Once upon a time, long ago, in a land far, far away, a wealthy man of incredible intellect came to live on a large island. Along with his natural intelligence, the man was also impressively educated.

The island was populated entirely by good-hearted but very average people. Because this man had money and academic degrees, because he seemed to know so much more about everything than anyone else who lived on the island, the residents there made him their de facto leader. Thus, they always deferred to his direction, his ideas, and his way of doing things.

"He knows every answer," the people said. "He is always correct. While we sometimes overlook what is right and true, he sees everything!"

Yes, that's exactly what they said: he sees everything. It was a curious way to describe the wealthy intellectual. For the man was completely blind.

Yes, the man's results *were* exceptional, and for a long time the results obtained by the islanders who doted on the man's leadership practically mirrored his own. Curiously, however, not a single person's results ever exceeded what the blind man accomplished. And, of course, because of the consistency of the rich man's results, the few problem areas that *did* exist were ignored.

Once, an islander did broach the subject of better results, asking how these problem areas might be improved. Their leader took a deep breath and simply explained the facts as he knew them—that in reality, nothing *could* be done.

"Not to boast," he added, "but remember, I know everything there is to know about this subject and this is just the way things are. It's sad, I know. But what I am telling you is absolutely true."

Also living on the island was an elder—a wise old gentleman—and he had overheard the rich man's reply to the islander's question. That night the old gentleman couldn't sleep, for the rich man's words bounced around in his head, repeating themselves over and over again. *Nothing can be done. I know everything there is to know. It's absolutely true.*

The next morning the wise old gentleman invited the rich man on an adventure to the other side of the island, promising to introduce him to something he had never experienced.

"There," he told the man, "lives a beast of immense proportions. You came from far away and so have never heard the beast described or even mentioned. Obviously, you are blind and cannot see the creature, but despite its size, it is very friendly. I will lead you close, and you will be able to touch it."

That afternoon, after a rather long journey, the two arrived at their destination. The elder carefully led the rich but blind man within a few feet of the beast. Speaking softly, the old man said, "He is directly in front of you. It is a most unusual animal that, as I mentioned, is also unusually large. It is known as an elephant."

Sensing the blind man's uneasiness, the wise elder calmly instructed, "Now, slowly, step forward and reach out. You will be able to feel him. After you do, please describe the animal as best you can and then, with your incredible intellect, tell me how the creature might be used."

With this instruction, the blind man raised his hands and moved forward tentatively. Touching the massive animal with his palms flat, he moved his hands slowly along its side. Right and left, up and down. Moving back to his right, he repeated the process before moving left and doing it again. Before long, a grin broke out on the blind man's face, prompting his old guide to ask, "Are you prepared to answer?"

"Yes," the blind man replied confidently. "An elephant is like a wall. It is a big, high, slightly curved but mostly flat, very roughly textured wall. An elephant could be used as a boundary or a large gate or perhaps as one part of a much longer wall."

When the elder remained silent, the blind man attempted to prompt confirmation. "Well?" he asked. "Am I correct? Is my description and list of uses true?"

"Yes," the wise old man nodded, "everything you said is true." Then he cocked his head and added, "It's just not the truth."

The blind man was shocked. "I don't understand," he said. "Not the truth? How could it even be possible to dispute my findings? How could my conclusion not be the truth?"

"There are two answers to that question," the elder replied. "One reveals the truth about the elephant. The other reveals the truth about you."

The rich man thought for a time before saying, "Okay. I am stumped. What is the truth about the elephant? And what do I not already know that could possibly be the truth about me?"

The wise old man placed his hand on the other's shoulder. With a smile in his voice, he gently said, "As regards the elephant, your hands and mind stopped exploring long before you understood the totality of the animal before you. Perhaps it is because you are so smart, but you quickly decided what the elephant was like, how he could be used, and without thinking beyond what you already knew, you immediately stated your answer.

"What you had learned is correct. What you stated is true. But you did not go as far as you could have gone. You never reached the foundation. Therefore, you do not—and cannot possibly—even comprehend the whole truth about an elephant."

"What should I have done?" the blind man asked.

"Had you continued only a few feet to your left," the wise elder responded, "you might have found the elephant like a snake or a flexible pipe that could be used to siphon water. By feeling down to the left or right, you could have declared the elephant akin to a set of strong columns able to be used as supports for a hut."

The rich man was about to speak, but the elder stopped him. Chuckling, the old man said, "Wait, there's more! While it is true that, at the back end, one could say the animal is like a flyswatter or paintbrush, and it is true that, at the other end, one could say he is like two big fans . . . the truth—the whole truth—is that the elephant is *all* of these things and probably more.

"In fact, if indeed there *is* more to the elephant, then all you and I know now is merely true, whereas the truth would be that foundation for which we must continue to strive."

The blind man was nodding, soaking in every word. Beginning to understand, he asked, "And what about the other answer? What is the truth about me?"

"The truth about you is simple," the elder replied. "There *is* more. There is more for you to learn and understand. There is more for you to become. Yes, you already know more than everyone else. That is true. But *the truth* is lying well beyond what you know."

The old man paused. Except for the faint breeze in the palms and the sounds of the birds, all was silent. The elephant, still very close, shifted his weight. The blind man heard the movement and smiled. He was pondering the old man's words, and he, too, was quiet.

He was waiting. Waiting for what, he was not sure, but somehow, he knew the old man was deep in thought as well . . . perhaps praying. He felt the old man gathering himself to finish what he wanted to say and sensed a desire for his words to be delivered perfectly.

The elder couldn't have known the blind man's thoughts, of course, but, in fact, he had said a short prayer. He did have something else to say. And he did want to deliver the words perfectly.

Knowing the importance of the concept he was explaining to this influential man, he wanted very much for the last thought he was about to deliver to be remembered. He intended that it engage the mind of this leader and that it pierce his heart.

Finally, he spoke.

"My friend," he began, "you are very smart. I also believe you to have great wisdom. This is why my people rely upon you. Now, however, the time has come for you to seek higher levels of understanding than you have ever known existed. You *must* do this for your children and the generations that will follow. You must do this for us—because we have chosen you as our example and inspiration."

Taking a deep breath, the wise old man finished the message that would ultimately impact millions. He said, "Finally, you must do this because you might be the only one who can. Our families are our lives. Our businesses support our families and bring value to others. We, the people who follow you, want to do well, to grow, to prosper. We don't mind working hard.

"But what a tragedy it would be if one day we are found to have achieved only average results produced by what is true . . . because the person upon whom we depended to lead us never bothered to pursue the truth."

Twenty-two

CONNECTING THE DOTS

Do you remember the dot-connecting game books we played with as children? The process was a simple one. Connecting dots in a numbered order was the only thing required to reveal a hidden image. "It's a giraffe!" we would yell. Or perhaps it was a palm tree or an airplane or the Statue of Liberty.

The dots laid out in *this* book—available now for you to connect—will reveal a pathway to the life you choose. But I must warn you, this is a pathway, not a shortcut. The dots waiting for you now—the dots that can create the framework of a successful life—correlate well to the game you played as a child.

Can you recall a time you skipped all over the paper, missing a few dots and doing the rest out of order? Remember how the result was a scribbly bunch of nothing? Well, the same result can be had here. You can choose only one dot—the one with which you are comfortable—and hammer it to death. Or you can pick a couple and move back and forth between them for years. And you will get *something*. But it won't be the family situation for which you are hoping. It won't be the business of your dreams. It won't be the life you might have lived.

Yes, whatever life you wish to lead waits for you in the dots we have found at the bottom of the pool. But they must be examined carefully and connected correctly. The lessons they contain must be fully understood and applied with consistency and generosity.

So let's review, shall we?

Obviously there are results on the surface, but the greatest results to be gained are accomplished by thinking to the deepest level of an issue. Kevin's swim to the bottom of the pool proved that the greatest results were to be had by harnessing the power of the foundation. And the foundation of anything is never in the middle or near the top.

Remember that when you head for the bottom, most around you will react skeptically or, occasionally, in an outright negative manner. But when you find and establish the location of the foundation, the results created will draw others to your efforts. These are the people with whom you can begin to create extraordinary results.

At this point your personal belief level in an incredible future is higher than ever before because you have experienced unusual results. The belief level of those around you is also high, primarily because they have seen your results. This small team with whom you are now surrounding yourself begins to act, work, and think with the benefit of that belief, and greater success is achieved (and compounded) by all.

Don't forget your sense of humor. Exercise it often. The most important leadership role you will ever undertake is the one of leading yourself. And as you lead yourself, do so with a controlled imagination.

A controlled imagination will not only connect dots that sometimes seem invisible to others; it will banish the fear that threatens your confidence and joy. Worry and doubt are products of fear. And fear is nothing more than a misuse of the imagination with which you have been created.

Do not mingle long with those proud souls who strut around outside their boxes. Instead, slip quietly and confidently past the rabble, moving in the direction known as *beyond*. When you find it, take a moment to celebrate before setting your sights again . . . on beyond.

Your life is like a grand game. If you decide there are no more moves, that there is no more beyond . . . if you decide you have arrived, the game is over.

Life's richest rewards are gained searching for wisdom. Wisdom is a deeper understanding of principle. After a deeper understanding is achieved, the only place to go is . . . deeper. Diamonds are seldom found lying on the ground. Diamonds are hidden deep within the earth. Similarly, wisdom only *seems* rare because most people attempt to gain it while remaining at the surface. A deeper understanding of principle—wisdom—waits for you at the bottom of the pool.

Your place of retreat—your Location of Contemplation—is not rental property. It cannot be loaned or stolen. You cannot be evicted. This mind palace is reserved for you, so decorate it as you wish and check in often. No prior notice is required. This is your fortress of solitude—the place for you to hope, dream, aim, rest, plan, question, design, wait, renew, celebrate, imagine, begin, and become.

There is danger in what is true, for most who find it cancel their search for anything beyond what they have already found. *Why continue,* they ask themselves? *This is the answer!* In this belief, however, they are mistaken. They have not found *the* answer. They have found *an* answer. There is a big difference between the two.

The danger, of course, exists in the fact that *an* answer—one that is true—is almost always accepted by the masses because it is logical and does indeed produce results. Thus, what is true becomes the default position of everyone who hears it explained or experiences its results.

What is the danger in that, you ask. None, if your intention—personally and professionally—is to move from *good* to *great*. But if your sights are set on going from great to *best*, you'll need more than what is merely true. You, my friend, will need the truth.

The following is an example of what is true on the surface while the truth quietly waits at the bottom of the pool.

For more than a generation, parents, teachers, coaches, authors, and speakers have propagated the idea that choices determine one's future. Nothing is more important, we are often told, than the choices we make. Speakers assert that your choices today dictate the life you will live tomorrow. "Make good choices!" we tell our children.

It all sounds so good, so right, so smart. Do you know why? Because choices *do* determine our future. That is a fact and absolutely true. But it is not the truth. Again, the truth about this—and about so many other things—waits for you at the bottom of the pool.

Question: Would you consider giving a coin to a child with the instructions to "flip heads every time," then, when the child was unable to accomplish that feat, punish him?

No?

Why not?

Because, you'd likely reply, landing heads every time one flips a coin is an impossible task.

And you'd be right. It *is* impossible. Therefore, it would be cruel to punish the child who couldn't do it. After all, if we as adults haven't figured out how to flip heads every time and understand that process well enough to explain it to the child, what chance would a child have of doing it?

I suppose, then, that if heads is the desired result, we all just will have to hope we can flip heads *most* of the time.

More questions: How beneficial is it to tell a child to make good choices? Is there a most effective number of times he must be told in order to get that message across? Have you ever known adults who made bad choices? Were they never told as children to make good ones? Did they not know their choices would determine their destinies?

Isn't telling a child to make good choices merely the equivalent of telling a child to flip heads every time? Could it be that, as adults, many of us have not figured out the truth about how good choices are made, much less understand the process well enough to explain it to a child?

And if that *is* the case—knowing full well that making good choices is the desired result for all of us—do we need to readjust our expectations? Do we simply need to hope we can make good choices most of the time?

No.

While, again, it is true that choices determine our future, the truth exists *below* choice, at a foundational level. What might be more foundational than choice?

Your *thinking*.

Your thinking—as far as your life's results go—is as bottom of the pool as you can get. Your choices may determine your destiny, but it is your thinking that determines your choices.

Just to be certain . . . if you ever doubt this critical fact, I'll urge you to remember that every choice you have ever made in your life, and every choice you'll ever make in the future, has been, and will be, totally determined by

- how you think,
- what you think,

- how long you think about it,
- what you decide you don't have time to think about
  so you aren't distracted from
  thinking about what you have to think about
  in order for you to be able to decide . . .

See what I mean? It's your thinking.

And because the bottom of the pool has revealed your thinking to be the actual foundation of the future you wish to create, you are now in for some very good news: your life will not be a coin flip after all.

If it is true that your choices determine your
destiny . . .
and if the truth is that your thinking determines
your choices . . .
then it is, in fact, your thinking that determines
your destiny.

But that's not even the exciting part.

In this particular case, the good news has to do with the fact that you were created with the ability to make choices. Therefore, we see God's greatest paradox revealed in our own lives. It goes like this: yes, your thinking determines your choices, but because you were created with the ability to make choices, you can choose how to think!

Okay, I just saw your brow furrow. I saw you cock your head, and I know what just ran through your mind. *Andy*, you are wondering, *I understand how my thinking determines my choices, but how is it possible to choose how I think?*

You can choose how you think because you choose the situations that form your thoughts.

Know this:

> ***How you think* is massively influenced and largely determined by what you read, hear, and watch.**

Another huge factor in forming the foundation of you is the group of people with whom you surround yourself. These people also have a great deal of sway upon what you read, hear, and watch.

Therefore, you can choose how you think because you can choose what you read. You can choose how you think because you can choose what you listen to and choose what you watch. You can also choose the people with whom you associate.

Perhaps *more important* to the process of choosing how you think is that you can choose what you will *not* read. You can choose what you will *not* listen to and choose what you will *not* watch. You can choose the people with whom you will *not* be around.

Years ago a case concerning the definition of pornography wound its way through the system before finally making it to the Supreme Court. The issue was argued in 1963 and was apparently so complicated that a decision was not rendered until fifteen months later in 1964. In the concurring opinion delivered by

Justice Potter Stewart, he famously wrote these words about the definition of pornography: "I know it when I see it."

Really? Thanks. That helps a lot.

Yeah, you laugh, but that official opinion by a justice of the United States Supreme Court continues to be the default definition still used today by America's educational systems, state and local governments, and private industry. In other words, even now, there is no definition. Whether print, film, or online content is or is not pornographic remains a judgment call. Thus, the definition of pornography varies wildly because the judgments rest solely upon the shoulders of whoever makes the call. And of course, they—like Justice Stewart in 1964—know it when they see it.

The bottom of the pool, however, provides hope that issues of this kind and many other types can be decided accurately. If you'd like a quick trip to the bottom of the pool right now, you and I will be able to define this particular issue with the truth once and for all, and in a way with which no one can argue or ever forget.

Remembering that the quality of our answers will be determined by the quality of our questions, let's begin with a good one.

If a person were to contrast photographs of naked people in magazine centerfolds with the statue of Venus de Milo or Michelangelo's *David*, what's the difference? They are all nude depictions of the human body. Why would the photographs be deemed pornography while the statues would universally be considered art?

Good questions. The answer is very simple. The difference in pornography and art is determined by what you think about as you look.

Therefore, in this and every other part of your life, know that your thinking prompts your choices. And because your choices are the building blocks of your future, be wise in how you choose to think.

Twenty-three

REACHING THE PROMISED LAND

For now, our time together is almost at an end, and I'm curious: Does what you say you want out of life line up well with your daily actions? In other words, do you *at least* do what you know to do?

I feel as though you and I have connected through these pages. Therefore, I don't mind telling you something I don't ordinarily reveal. My personal answer to the question above—Does what you say you want out of life line up well with your daily actions?—has changed through the years.

There was a time in my life when my honest answer would have been no. I did not even do the things I *knew* to do. Yes, I felt horrible about it, but I seemed stuck. And the more I *thought* about it, the *less* I did. My dreams seemed ridiculously out of reach, beyond the realm of possibility. Why? Because I knew myself too well. I talked a good game but played without enthusiasm, effort, or hope.

During that time, at least I did continue to think about my lack of action. Mostly I thought about it in a negative way, but I did indeed think about it. And before too many years had passed, there came a time when I was able to say "I'm not a *no* anymore. I have graduated to a *sometimes*."

I had reached a point, at least, when I knew that *sometimes* I was doing and working and acting in a way that moved my life forward. The life I wanted for my family was not only coming into focus but also appeared closer than I had ever before been able to imagine.

Today I would tell you that I am a *mostly*. I'd love to be an *always*, but, frankly, I just haven't gotten there yet. Mostly, however, I am able to do what I am supposed to do and act like I am supposed to act in order to live the life I want to live. And I am able to accomplish this moderate level of successful being because I have become pretty good at choosing the way I think.

Pretty good. My thought process ranges above a "sometimes" and below an "always." Yep, I'm a "mostly."

I also want you to know that books of the type you are reading now used to drive me nuts. "You HAVE to read this!" someone would tell me about something they had just read ten times. "This book," they would say very seriously, "will change everything in your life!"

During my years of uncertainty, I actually did read some of them, but not a one ever changed my life.

Now that I think about it, I hope no one told you that *this* book will change *everything* in *your* life. Because it won't.

Changing everything in your life? That's going to be up to you. Up. To. You.

You see, an excellent book is like an excellent hammer. Books are tools. A book never changed anyone's life any more than a hammer ever built anyone's house. Of course, a person who never learned to use a hammer never built a house either. My point is that certain books provide an education or a measure of understanding that cannot be gained anywhere else or in any other way.

Yeah, I know the whole "up to you" thing seems scary—maybe even impossible at the moment. Fortunately it's a message that carries great news: because the life you intend to live *is* up to you, there exists hope and control that would not otherwise be the case. If the life you want to lead was up to someone or something else—your spouse, a coworker, the government, a neighbor, the economy, a hurricane—then you'd have zero control and very little hope.

However, while you cannot control many of the situations you face in life, you can control how you respond when tough circumstances occur. If you can understand and believe that *bad* thinking can lead to *bad* choices, and that, in turn, those *bad* choices yield *bad* life situations, then surely you can understand and believe that *good* thinking can lead to *good* choices, and that, in turn, your *good* choices will yield *great* life situations.

Again, your thinking is the root system that will feed the personal growth needed in order for your life to align with every God-given hope and dream you have. And because you have been created with the ability to choose your thinking, you have been created with the ability to choose your destiny. Knowing this and remembering this will allow you to consistently maintain a high degree of hope—for the future you desire is within your grasp.

Do you have the breath for one last subject? Can we stay at the bottom of the pool for just a bit longer? Good. I only have a few more questions:

1. When you imagine, what do you imagine?
2. What is the relationship between THE BEST and THE TRUTH? Have you ever considered the fact that you can know THE TRUTH but because of a lack of discipline or a selfish spirit still never approach anything near THE BEST? Yet can you accomplish THE BEST without knowing THE TRUTH?
3. Who is the author of truth? Is it you? Me? If neither of us is the author of truth, are we still able to search for the truth and find it?
4. While searching for the truth, might it be helpful to also search for its Author?
5. Did you know there exists a difference between "the best one can imagine" and THE BEST?
6. Who has a better imagination? . . . You—or the Creator of the universe?

7. If you want the best for you and your Creator wants the best for you . . . when *you* imagine the best for you and your Creator imagines the best for you, how big is the gap in between?

I ask these seven questions for a simple reason. Before I reveal that reason, I want you to know *that I know* that you are an intelligent person. I feel certain that you comprehend everything you've read in these pages. You understood the bottom of the pool metaphor immediately and have probably found the truth beyond true several times already.

Please know that I very much appreciate you having read this book. I'm honored to have (hopefully) furnished a few of the small building blocks you will use in the construction of your very large future.

Now to the reason for the seven questions: while I have seen companies, teams, and organizations use the material we have discussed to create influence, peace in relationships, rescue for others, and wealth, I have also seen people refuse to harness their thinking.

In previous chapters (more than once), I have referred to those who "just don't want to think that hard." Knowing that one's thinking is the foundation of everything that comes after, seeing someone shut down—refusing to contemplate, ponder, muse, or imagine—has been one of the saddest experiences of my life. And I refuse to experience it with you.

Therefore, I hereby declare and decree that you will enjoy the benefits of a lifetime spent contemplating, pondering, and musing. You will consistently harness that powerful imagination you own to explore the bottom of the pool.

Final Note

I awakened this morning at three o'clock and was unable to go back to sleep. Frankly, you were on my mind. Polly was breathing softly as I eased out of our bedroom, grabbed a glass of water in the kitchen, and slipped out the back door. I paused in the quiet darkness before descending the outside stairs to my office. I wanted to finish this final chapter with something personal . . . perhaps one last example of choosing how we think.

6:10

It is getting light outside my office window. A hint of red is showing in the eastern sky.

6:15

The sky is beginning to lighten. There is also quite a bit more color than there was just a few minutes ago. I'm not sure whether you've considered the difference, but a sunrise is more valuable than a sunset. Remember the connections we've made between value and rarity? Sunrises are rare events.

"Wait a minute," someone might say. "Both appear once every day. Sunrises are not any rarer than sunsets. There are exactly the same number of each."

6:18

Okay . . . that makes sense if that's how someone else chooses to think. You and I, however, choose to think about the difference between the two like this:

> Everyone sees sunsets. Because everyone is awake when they happen. Glance at the western sky toward the end of the day. There. You saw another one. As breathtaking as they can be, sunsets are created when the sun is down. Sunsets are a sign that the day is done.

6:19

If only because most people won't get out of bed to experience the dawn of a new day, sunrises are rare. By the way, though I am alone at the moment, I am proclaiming what is about to happen to be your sunrise.

6:21

And there it is. Incredible . . . complete with reds and purples of every shade and intensity. Whites and yellows swirl with fiery pinks as all of it plays against the background of sapphire brightening on the horizon. As the dark cobalt of last night's sky disappears, the sunrise spills its full measure of promise into the very first heartbeat of this day, declaring a fresh start and reminding you of the opportunity that exists in your future.

It is often said that at the end of their lives, most people imagine what might have been. That's very likely the case. But only because, at the beginning, very few people take the time to imagine what their lives might one day become.

Most wait for the sunset. Few get up for the sunrise. You are not "most." You are among the few. Today's sunrise is unique in pattern and color, but it possesses the same message that will be delivered to you by every sunrise that follows. The message that this is the beginning.

Sunrises proclaim the future, not the past. They bring assurance, not uncertainty. A sunrise is the onset, not the outcome; the potential, never the limit. And while sunsets are for everyone, from this moment forward . . .

All sunrises belong to you.

ABOUT THE AUTHOR

Hailed by a *New York Times* reporter as "someone who has quietly become one of the most influential people in America," Andy Andrews is a bestselling novelist, speaker, and consultant for some of the world's most successful teams, largest corporations, and fastest-growing organizations. Listeners in almost one hundred countries have subscribed to his weekly podcast, *The Professional Noticer*, on AndyAndrews.com/podcast and other sites that offer podcast subscriptions.

Andy is also the creator of WisdomHarbour.com—a portal that is fast becoming one of the most shared websites of the decade. He has spoken at the request of four United States presidents and works closely with America's Special Operations Command.

Zig Ziglar said, "Andy Andrews is the best speaker I have ever seen."

Andy is the author of the *New York Times* bestsellers *The Noticer*, *How Do You Kill 11 Million People?*, and the modern classic *The Traveler's Gift*—which has sold millions of copies worldwide.

He lives in Orange Beach, Alabama, with his wife, Polly, and their two sons.

The PROFESSIONAL NOTICER

Observations and Answers with Andy Andrews

AVAILABLE WHEREVER YOU LISTEN TO YOUR PODCASTS.

IF YOU HAVE A QUESTION YOU WOULD LIKE ANDY TO ANSWER ON **THE PROFESSIONAL NOTICER**, PLEASE CONTACT US AT:

1-800-726-ANDY
THEPROFESSIONALNOTICER@ANDYANDREWS.COM

The
LITTLE
THINGS
ANDY
ANDREWS

ANDY
ANDREWS
The
NOTICER
RETURNS